Conservation of... what?

CW00740457

Many times in physics you will make use of the conservation idea. T
but turns out to be very powerful. In everyday language, it comes do
'Whatever you start out with, you must end up with.'
Whatever changes may have happened along the way and whatever 'disguises' might be
involved, the conservation idea remains true.

Newton's cradle is a good example. Once you have provided the initial energy to set the balls in
motion, then the total energy in the system remains the same whenever you calculate its value.
Some energy will appear as kinetic energy, some as potential energy, and some as heat energy or
sound energy, but the total will always be the same.

Therefore if you ever add up the total and some energy is 'missing', then you know you haven't
thought about *all* the energy transfers going on and it prompts you to look a little more closely,
perhaps discovering something you hadn't known before. Geiger and Marsden made a critical
discovery about the structure of atoms when they noticed that the numbers in their experiment
didn't quite add up.

There are other conservation rules. For example, we use ideas about *conservation of mass.* In
almost any change, the total number of atoms at the end must be the same as at the start, and at
one time this was thought to be always true. They might be rearranged into complicated new
patterns or new states, but all the particles must be there. For example, think about what
a tree is made from. Combining atoms, making sure that we account for all of them, allows us to
'build' the tree. Using just carbon dioxide from the air, water from the soil and traces of other
simple chemicals, the atoms combine to form the largest living things ever seen on the Earth.

But physics is also a developing science – it is not finished! During the development of nuclear
physics in the 20th century, careful experiments showed that in some situations mass was *not*
conserved and neither was the energy. Atoms can even appear and disappear.
Mass seemed to appear from nowhere and energy disappeared altogether.
A deeper truth was revealing itself and now, in some situations, we need to
make use of the full conservation rule, the *conservation of mass-energy.*
A rule that involves the most famous physics equation of them all:

$$E = mc^2$$

Albert Einstein (1879 – 1955).
Although famous for his papers on special and
general relativity, he won the 1921 Nobel Prize for
Physics for his work on the photoelectric effect.

William Collins' dream of knowledge for all began with the publication of his first book in 1819. A self-educated mill worker, he not only enriched millions of lives, but also founded a flourishing publishing house.

Today, staying true to this spirit, Collins books are packed with inspiration, innovation and practical expertise. They place you at the centre of a world of possibility and give you exactly what you need to explore it.

Collins
DO MORE

This high quality material is endorsed by Edexcel and has been through a rigorous quality assurance programme to ensure that it is a suitable companion to the specification for both learners and teachers.

This does not mean that its contents will be used verbatim when setting examinations nor is it to be read as being the official specification – a copy of which is available at **www.edexcel.org.uk**

Published by Collins
An imprint of HarperCollinsPublishers
77–85 Fulham Palace Road,
Hammersmith,
London W6 8JB

Browse the complete Collins Education catalogue at
www.collinseducation.com

©HarperCollinsPublishers Limited 2006

10 9 8 7 6 5 4 3

ISBN-10: 0-00-775547-3
ISBN-13: 978-0-00-775547-3

Malcolm Bradley asserts his moral right
to be identified as the author of this work

All rights reserved. No part of this publication may be reproduced, stored in a retrieval system, or transmitted in any form or by any means, electronic, mechanical, photocopying, recording or otherwise, without the prior written permission of the Publisher or a licence permitting restricted copying in the United Kingdom issued by the Copyright Licensing Agency Ltd., 90 Tottenham Court Road, London W1T 4LP

British Library Cataloguing in Publication Data
A Catalogue record for this publication is available from the British Library

Cover design by White-Card, London
Additional text by Tim Jolly
Text page design by Christina Newman
New artwork by Jerry Fowler

Printed and bound by Martins the Printers, Berwick upon Tweed

IGCSE for Edexcel
PHYSICS

by Malcolm Bradley

Collins

CONTENTS

GETTING THE BEST FROM THE BOOK

Welcome to *IGCSE Physics for Edexcel*. This textbook and the accompanying CD-ROM have been designed to help you understand all of the requirements needed to succeed in the Edexcel IGCSE Physics course. Just as there are seven sections in the Edexcel syllabus so there are seven sections in the textbook: Forces and motion, Electricity, Waves, Energy resources and energy transfer, Solids, liquids and gases, Magnetism and electromagnetism, and Radioactivity and particles. Each section in the book covers the essential knowledge and skills you need. The textbook also has some very useful features that have been designed to help you understand all the aspects of Physics that you will need to know for this specification.

Coverage of each topic is linked closely to the Edexcel specification so that you build a powerful knowledge-base with which to succeed in the examination.

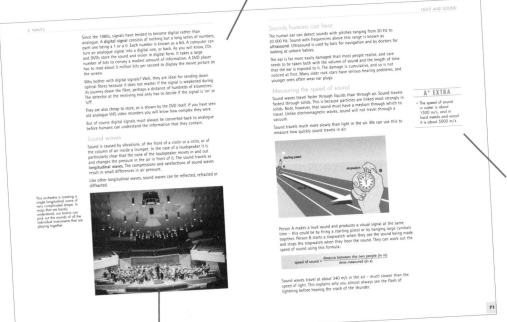

This section has been designed to challenge those who want to achieve the very top grades. The A* extra feature is normally an extra piece of information or a tip.

Photographic images really help in visualising the information you need.

There will be two stages to your assessment on the course because Edexcel IGCSE Physics is assessed in the following manner:

Paper 1 – Examination 1F – The Foundation Tier, worth 80% of the marks

OR

Paper 2 – Examination 2H – The Higher Tier, worth 80% of the marks.

AND

Paper 3 – This examination is designed to test skills in experimental physics – common to both tiers, worth 20% of the marks

OR

Paper 4 – Coursework – common to both tiers, worth 20% of the marks.

Collins *IGCSE Physics for Edexcel* covers all of the topics and skills you will need to achieve success, whichever assessment pathway you are entered for.

Lots of clear illustrations to help you simplify and understand the complexities of physical processes in the physical world.

To be able to do well in the subject you will need to know how to complete physical calculations. The worked examples in the text take you through the question step by step to help you really understand.

Banks of questions appear after every topic to test your understanding of the work you've just covered. All the answers can be found using the information in the text.

IGCSE Physics CD-ROM

To help you through the course we have added this unique CD-ROM, which you may be able to use in class or as part of your private study. To allow you to understand the subject as you progress through the course we have added the following features to the CD-ROM.

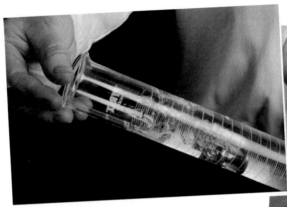

LIST OF VIDEOS ON THE PHYSICS CD-ROM
1. Different energy types
2. Mass + weight + momentum
3. Hooke's law
4. Constant velocity
5. $F = ma$
6. Electrostatics
7. The volume and density of an irregular shape
8. Terminal velocity
9. Pressure
10. Circuits
11. Simple parallel circuit
12. Iron filings/compass
13. Making an electromagnet
14. Making a motor/Faraday motor
15. Heat: thermal expansion and contraction
16. Types of heat transfer
17. The spectrum
18. Ray boxes/Reflection with mirrors
19. Refraction, reflection, diffraction
20. Radioactivity

VIDEO CLIPS

Physics is a practical subject and to reinforce your studies the CD-ROM includes 20 short films that demonstrate experiments and practical work. Each of the films covers an area that you need to know well for the practical section of the course. The information in the films will also help you with the knowledge required in other parts of the specification. You can use the films to help you understand the topic you are currently studying or perhaps come back to them when you want to revise for the exam. Each of the films has sound too, so if you are watching them in a library or quiet study area you may need headphones.

QUESTION BANK

'Practice makes perfect', the saying goes, and we have included a large bank of questions related to the Physics specification to help you understand the topics you will be studying.

As with the films, your teacher may use this in class or you may want to try the questions in your private study sessions.

These questions will reinforce the knowledge you have gained in the classroom and through using the textbook, and could also be used when you are revising for your examinations. Don't try to do all the questions at once though; the most effective way to use this feature is by trying some of the questions every now and then to test yourself. In this way you will know where you need to do a little more work. The questions are not full 'exam-type' questions that you will be set by your IGCSE examiners. Some of the questions test underlying principles that are not specifically mentioned in your specification.

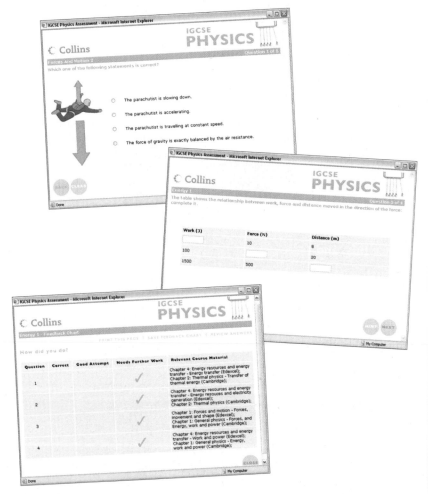

Good luck with your IGCSE Physics studies. This book and the CD-ROM provide you with stimulating, interesting and motivating learning resources that we are sure will help you succeed in your Physics course.

OPERATING SYSTEMS REQUIRED AND SET-UP INSTRUCTIONS

Mac system requirements
500 MHz PowerPC G3 and later
Mac OS X 10.1.x and above
128 MB RAM
Microsoft Internet Explorer 5.2, Firefox 1.x, Mozilla 1.x, Netscape 7.x and above, Opera 6, or Safari 1.x and above (Mac OS X 10.2.x only)
325 MB of free hard disc space

To run the program from the CD
1 Insert the CD into the drive.
2 When the CD icon appears on the desktop, double-click it.
3 Double-click Collins IGCSE Physics.html

To install the program to run from the hard drive
1 Insert the CD into the drive
2 When the CD icon appears on the desktop, double-click it to open a Finder window
3 Drag Collins IGCSE Physics.html to the desktop.
4 Drag Collins IGCSE Physics Content to the desktop.

PC system requirements
450 MHz Intel Pentium II processor (or equivalent) and later
Windows 98/ME/NT/2000/XP
128 MB RAM
Microsoft Internet Explorer 5.5, Firefox 1.x, Mozilla 1.x, Netscape 7.x and above, Opera 7.11 and above
325 MB of hard disc space

To run the program from the CD
1 Insert the CD into the drive.
2 Double-click on the CD-ROM drive icon inside My Computer.
3 Double-click Collins IGCSE Physics.html.

To install the program to run from the hard drive
1 Insert the disc into the drive.
2 Double-click the CD-ROM drive icon inside My Computer.
3 Double-click the SETUP.EXE.
4 Follow the onscreen instructions. These include instructions concerning the Macromedia Flash Player included with and required by the program.
5 When the installation is complete, remove the CD from the drive.

For free technical support, call our helpline on: + 44 141 306 3322 or send an email to it.helpdesk@harpercollins.co.uk

Completed in 2003, Taipei 101 (because it has 101 floors) holds the 'world's tallest' in several categories, such as the highest occupied floor and the world's fastest elevators, rising from the basement to the 89th floor in 39 seconds

101st floor

The 87th floor holds a 900-ton tuned-mass damper to counteract earthquakes

Reaching for the sky

Have you ever wondered just how much physics is involved in building a tall building?

For a start, think about some of the forces. Gravity is trying to pull your building down so you must use materials that have enough strength to balance this, and what you use to join them together must be just as strong. But don't forget the wind! The wind is trying to turn your building over sideways; your design will have to withstand considerable turning effects. And what about inside the building? You need to create lots of space so the building is useful. You will need to know about forces and how to control them.

People need to get about inside the building too. You will need some elevators, but how long will these take to reach the top? People won't want to spend an hour reaching their floor. So how fast can an elevator travel and how quickly can it accelerate without making the people inside feel ill? You are going to need to know about motion.

FORCES AND MOTION

The Petronas Towers in Kuala Lumpur.
Completed in 1998

88th floor

'Sky bridge' connects the two buildings
at the 41st and 42nd floors

The world's deepest foundations,
reaching 120 m down to bedrock

MOVEMENT AND POSITION

Videos & questions on the CD ROM

We have all been in a car travelling at 90 kilometres per hour. This, of course, means that the car (if it kept travelling at this speed for one hour) would travel 90 km. During one second of its journey this car travels 25 metres, so its speed can also be described as 25 metres per second. Scientists prefer to measure time in seconds, and distance in metres. So they prefer to measure speed in metres per second, often written as m/s.

Using graphs to study motion: distance–time graphs

Journeys can be summarised using **graphs**. The simplest type is a **distance–time graph** where the distance travelled is plotted against the time of the journey.

At the beginning of an experiment, time is usually given as 0 s, and the position of the object 0 m. If the object is not moving, then time increases, but distance does not. This gives a horizontal line. If the object is travelling at a steady speed, then both time and distance increase steadily, which gives a straight line. If the speed is varying, then the line will not be straight.

A distance–time graph for a bicycle. The graph slopes when the bicycle is moving. The slope gets steeper when the bicycle goes faster. The slope is straight (has a constant gradient) when the bicycle's speed is constant. After the cyclist falls off 150 m from the start, the graph is horizontal because the bicycle is not moving.

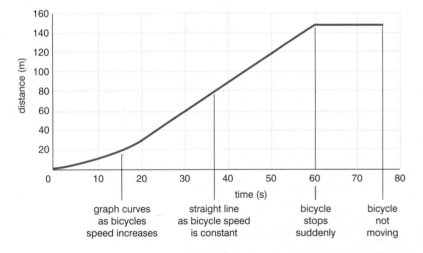

| graph curves as bicycles speed increases | straight line as bicycle speed is constant | bicycle stops suddenly | bicycle not moving |

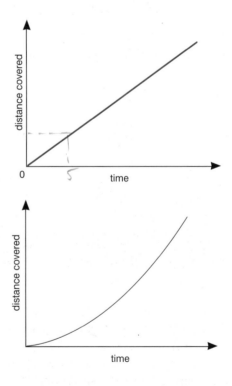

Steady speed is shown by a straight line. Steady increase in speed is shown by a smooth curve.

Calculating average speed

The **speed** of an object can be calculated using the following formula:

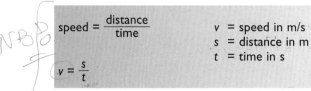

$$speed = \frac{distance}{time}$$

v = speed in m/s
s = distance in m
t = time in s

$$v = \frac{s}{t}$$

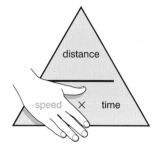

distance

speed × time

Cover speed to find that
$$speed = \frac{distance}{time}$$

Most objects speed up and slow down as they travel. An object's 'average speed' can be calculated by dividing the total distance travelled by the total time taken.

WORKED EXAMPLES

1 Calculate the average speed of a car that travels 500 m in 20 seconds.

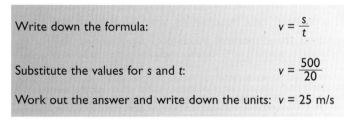

Write down the formula:	$v = \dfrac{s}{t}$
Substitute the values for s and t:	$v = \dfrac{500}{20}$
Work out the answer and write down the units:	$v = 25$ m/s

2 A horse canters at an average speed of 5 m/s for 2 minutes. Calculate the distance it travels.

Write down the formula in terms of s:	$s = v \times t$
Substitute the values for v and t:	$s = 5 \times 2 \times 60$
Work out the answer and write down the units:	$s = 600$ m

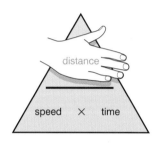

distance

speed × time

Cover distance to find that
distance = speed × time

Each car's average speed can be calculated by dividing the distance it has travelled by the time it has taken.

ARE SPEED AND VELOCITY THE SAME?

There are many situations in which we want to know the direction that an object is travelling. For example, when a space rocket is launched, it is likely to reach a speed of 1000 km/h after about 30 seconds. However, it is extremely important to know whether this speed is upwards or downwards. You want to know the speed *and* the direction of the rocket. The velocity of an object is one piece of information, but it consists of two parts: the speed and the direction. In this case, the velocity of the rocket is 278 m/s (its speed) upwards (its direction).

A velocity can have a minus sign. This tells you that the object is travelling in the opposite direction. So a velocity of –278 m/s upwards is actually a velocity of 278 m/s downwards.

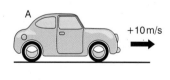

Both cars have the same speed. Car A has a velocity of +10 m/s, car B has a velocity of –10 m/s.

Calculating acceleration

If the speedometer of a car displays 50 km/h, and then a few seconds later it displays 70 km/h, then the car is accelerating. If the car is slowing down, this is called negative acceleration, or <u>deceleration</u>.

Let us imagine that the car is initially travelling at 15 m/s, and that one second later it has reached 17 m/s, and that its speed increases by 2 m/s each second after that. Each second its speed increases by 2 metres per second. We can say that its speed is increasing at '2 metres per second *per second*'. This can be written, much more conveniently, as an acceleration of 2 m/s².

Our planet Earth attracts all objects towards its centre with the force of gravity. The strength of the force decreases slowly with distance from the surface of the Earth, but for objects within a few km of the surface, all objects that are falling freely will have the same constant acceleration of just under 10 m/s². If a coconut falls from a tree, then after 1 s it will be falling at 10 m/s (though it will only have travelled 5 m because, of course, it started with zero velocity). After 2 s it will be falling at 20 m/s, if it does not hit the ground first.

How much an object's **speed or velocity changes** in a certain time is its **acceleration**. Acceleration can be calculated using the following formula:

A* EXTRA

• A negative acceleration shows that the object is slowing down.

$$\text{acceleration} = \frac{\text{change in velocity}}{\text{time taken}}$$

$$a = \frac{(v - u)}{t}$$

a = acceleration

v = final velocity in m/s

u = starting velocity in m/s

t = time in s

WORKED EXAMPLE

Calculate the acceleration of a car that travels from 0 m/s to 28 m/s in 10 seconds.

Write down the formula:	$a = \dfrac{(v - u)}{t}$
Substitute the values for v, u and t:	$a = \dfrac{(28 - 0)}{10}$
Work out the answer and write down the units:	$a = 2.8$ m/s²

Using velocity–time graphs

A **velocity–time graph** provides information on velocity, acceleration and distance travelled.

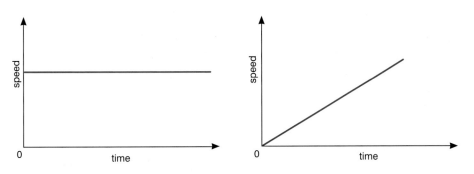

Steady speed is shown by a horizontal line. Steady acceleration is shown by a straight line sloping up.

In the graph above left, the object is already moving when the graph begins. If the object starts with a speed of zero, then the line starts from the origin.

Note that the object may not move to begin with. In this case the line will start by going along the time axis, showing that the speed stays at zero for a while.

Finding distance from a velocity–time graph

The area under a velocity–time graph gives you the distance travelled, because distance = velocity × time. Always make sure the units are consistent, velocity if the speed is in km/h, you must use time in hours too.

The graph below shows a car travelling between two sets of traffic lights. It can be divided into three regions.

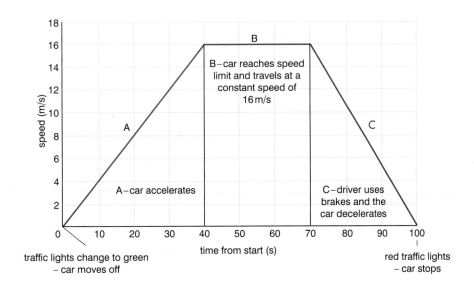

A velocity–time graph for a car travelling between two sets of traffic lights.

In region A, the car is **accelerating at a constant rate** (the line has a constant positive gradient). The distance travelled by the car can be calculated:

average velocity $= \dfrac{(16 + 0)}{2} = 8$ m/s

time $= 40$ s

so distance $= v \times t = 8 \times 40 = 320$ m

This can also be calculated from the area under the line
($\frac{1}{2}$ base $\times$ height $= \frac{1}{2} \times 40 \times 16 = 320$ m).

In region B, the car is travelling at a **constant speed** (the line has a gradient of zero). The distance travelled by the car can be calculated:

velocity $= 16$ m/s

time $= 30$ s

so distance $= v \times t = 16 \times 30 = 480$ m

This can also be calculated from the area under the line
(base $\times$ height $= 30 \times 16 = 480$ m).

In region C, the car is **decelerating at a constant rate** (the line has a constant negative gradient). The distance travelled by the car can be calculated:

average velocity $= \dfrac{(16 + 0)}{2} = 8$ m/s

time $= 30$ s

so distance $= v \times t = 8 \times 30 = 240$ m

This can also be calculated from the area under the line
($\frac{1}{2}$ base $\times$ height $= \frac{1}{2} \times 30 \times 16 = 240$ m).

In the above example, the acceleration and deceleration were constant, and the lines in regions A and C were straight. This is very often not the case. You will probably have noticed that a car can accelerate much more quickly when it is travelling at 30 km/h than it can when it is already travelling at 120 km/h.

A people-carrying space rocket does exactly the opposite, and if you watch one being launched you can see that it accelerates very slowly to begin with. As it is burning several tonnes of fuel per second, it quickly becomes lighter and starts to accelerate more quickly.

The velocity-time graphs we have used refer to motion in a straight line. In these graphs a change of velocity will mean a change of speed.

REVIEW QUESTIONS

Q1 Jane cycles to her friend's house. In the first part of her journey, she rides 200 m from her house to a road junction in 20 s. After waiting for 10 s to cross the road, Jane cycles for 20 s at 8 m/s to reach her friend's house.
  a What is Jane's average speed for the first part of the journey?
  b How far is it from the road junction to her friend's house?
  c What is Jane's average speed for the whole journey?

Q2 The graph shows a distance–time graph for a journey.
  a What does the graph tell us about the speed of the car between 20 and 60 seconds?
  b How far did the car travel between 20 and 60 seconds?
  c Calculate the speed of the car between 20 and 60 seconds.
  d What happened to the car between 80 and 100 seconds?

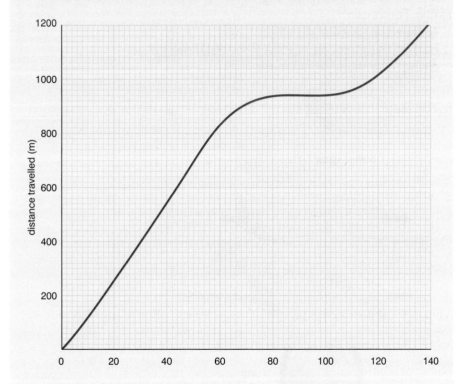

Q3 Look at the velocity–time graph for a toy tractor.
  a Calculate the acceleration of the tractor from A to B.
  b Calculate the total distance travelled by the tractor from A to C.

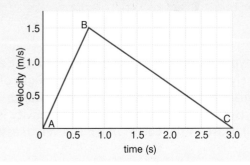

More questions on the CD ROM

FORCES, MOVEMENT AND SHAPE

Videos & questions on the CD ROM

What are forces?

A force is a push or a pull. The way that an object behaves depends on all of the forces acting on it. A force may come from the pull of a chain or rope, the push of a jet engine, the push of a pillar holding up a ceiling, and the pull of the gravitational field around the Earth.

EFFECTS OF FORCES

It is unusual for a single force to be acting on an object. Usually there will be two or more. The size and direction of these forces determine whether the object will move and the direction it will move in.

Forces are measured in **newtons** (N). They take many forms and have many effects including pushing, pulling, bending, stretching, squeezing and tearing. Forces can:
* **change the speed** of an object
* **change the direction** of movement of an object
* **change the shape** of an object.

Combinations of forces can have all kinds of effects.

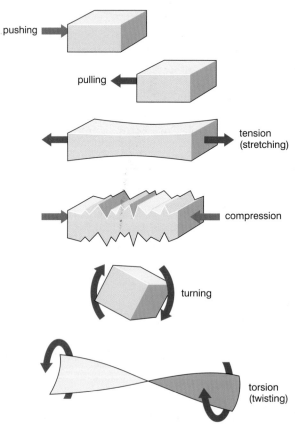

pushing

pulling

tension (stretching)

compression

turning

torsion (twisting)

Types of force

There are several different types of force. All objects in the universe attract each other with the extremely feeble force of gravity. The strength of the attraction depends on the mass of the two objects and the distance between the centres of the two objects. You may think that gravity is strong, but you are, after all, close to the Earth, which is a very massive object!

Electricity and magnetism both generate forces that are far stronger than gravity. You see magnetic forces being used every day when an electric motor turns.

There are a few other types of force apart from these three, for example the 'strong' force that is responsible for holding the nucleus of the atom together. But most of the forces that we feel or notice around us are one of the above three: gravitational, electrostatic or magnetic.

Electrostatic forces are the most important in our everyday lives. The reason that you are not sinking into the floor at the moment is that the electrons on the outside of the atoms of your shoes are being repelled by the electrons on the outside of the atoms on the floor. The same force is used when your hand lifts something up, or when friction slows down a car. In fact all of the forces in this section are either gravitational or – ultimately – electrostatic.

And when you consider that it is an electrostatic force that allows a bullet-proof coat to stop a speeding bullet, you'll probably agree that electrostatic forces are much stronger than gravity.

What is friction?

Friction is a very common force. It is the force that tries to stop movement between touching surfaces by opposing the movement.

In many situations friction can be a disadvantage, e.g. friction in the bearings of a bicycle wheel. In other situations, friction can be an advantage, e.g. between brake pads and a bicycle wheel.

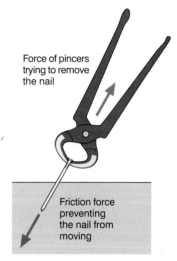

Force of pincers trying to remove the nail

Friction force preventing the nail from moving

Friction can stop any movement occurring at all, and it is friction that stops a nail coming out of a piece of wood.

Scalars and vectors

Force, velocity and acceleration are examples of **vector** quantities. A vector has a specific direction as well as a size, with a unit. We will meet many more later in this book: pressure, electrical current and even the flow of heat are all vectors.

Speed and mass are examples of **scalar** quantities. A scalar quantity has size only, with a unit. There are many more scalar quantities to be met: temperature, work, power and electrical resistance are all scalars.

To add vectors, draw them to scale, joining them in turn 'head to tail'. The final, or **resultant**, vector is drawn from the 'tail' of the first vector to the 'head' of the last one.

resultant vector

A* EXTRA

- Displacement is the vector quantity linked to distance, which is a scalar quantity. Displacement is the distance travelled *in a particular direction.*

The resultant vector represents the combined effect of the individual vectors.

The vector nature of force

To describe a force fully, you must state the size of the force and also the direction in which it is trying to move the object. The direction can be described in many different ways such as 'left to right', 'upwards' or 'north'. Sometimes it is useful to describe all of the forces in one direction as positive, and all of the forces in the other direction as negative. For two forces to be equal they must have the same size and the same direction.

Adding forces

If two or more forces are pulling or pushing an object in the same direction, then the effect of the forces will add up; if they are pulling it in opposite directions, then the backwards forces can be subtracted.

The husky dogs are able to pull the sledge due to the low level of friction between the sledge and the snow.

Twelve husky dogs are pulling a sledge. The sledge is travelling to the right and each dog is pulling with a force of 50 N. There is a friction force of 250 N that is trying to slow the sledge, and therefore must be pointing to the left.

The total force to the right is (12 × 50) N = 600 N.
The total force to the left is 250 N.
The **resultant** force (the total added-up force) = 600 – 250 N to the right
                                                        = 350 N to the right.

Note that you must give the direction of the net force.

BALANCED FORCES

Usually there are at least two forces acting on an object. If these two forces are **balanced** then the object will either be stationary or moving at a constant speed.

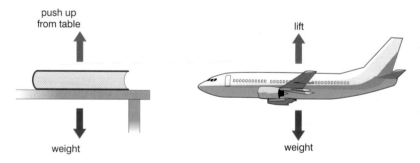

The book is stationary because the push upwards from the table equals the force of gravity downwards. If the table stopped pushing upwards, the book would fall.

This airplane is flying 'straight and level' because the lift generated by the air flowing over the wings is equal and opposite to the weight of the airplane. This diagram shows that the plane will neither climb nor dive, as it would if the forces were not equal.

A spacecraft in deep space will have no forces acting on it – no air resistance (no air), no force of gravity – and because there is no need to produce a forward force from its rockets, it will travel at a constant speed.

UNBALANCED FORCES

For an object's speed or direction of movement to change, the forces acting on it must be **unbalanced**.

As a gymnast first steps on to a trampoline, his weight is much greater than the opposing supporting force of the trampoline, so he moves downwards, stretching the trampoline. As the trampoline stretches, its supporting force increases until the supporting force is equal to the gymnast's weight. When the two forces are balanced, the trampoline stops stretching. If an elephant stood on the trampoline, it would break because it could never produce a supporting force equal to the elephant's weight.

You see the same effect if you stand on snow or soft ground. If you stand on quicksand, then the supporting force will not equal your weight, and you will continue to sink.

A trampoline stretches until it supports the weight on it.

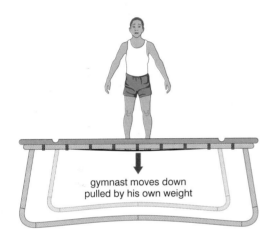

gymnast moves down pulled by his own weight

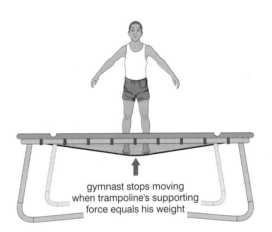

gymnast stops moving when trampoline's supporting force equals his weight

How are mass, force and acceleration related?

The acceleration of an object depends on its **mass** and the **force** that is applied to it. The relationship between these factors is given by the formula:

force = mass × acceleration	F = force in newtons
$F = ma$	m = mass in kg
	a = acceleration in m/s^2

This equation explains the definition of the newton. 'A newton is the force that will accelerate a mass of 1 kg at 1 m/s^2.'

The equation is perhaps easier to understand if we rearrange it into the form $a = \frac{F}{m}$. This shows us that if we use a big force we will get a larger acceleration, but if the object has more mass then we get a smaller acceleration.

So a light object with a large force applied to it will accelerate very fast. (Think of an athlete with a racing bicycle.) But a massive object with a small force applied to it will accelerate very slowly. (Think of a small child trying to pedal a large bicycle rickshaw.)

A* EXTRA

- The equation $F = ma$ shows that the acceleration of an object is directly proportional to the force acting (if its mass is constant) and is inversely proportional to its mass (if the force is constant). The gradient of a force–acceleration graph gives the mass of the object.

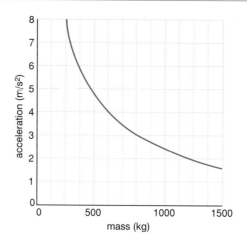

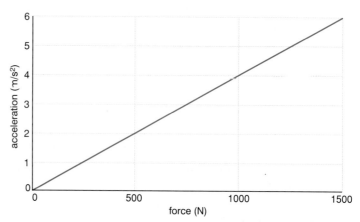

Acceleration is inversely proportional to mass and directly proportional to force.

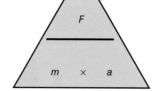

WORKED EXAMPLES

1 What force would be required to give a mass of 5 kg an acceleration of 10 m/s²?

Write down the formula:	$F = ma$
Substitute the values for m and a:	$F = 5 \times 10$
Work out the answer and write down the units:	$F = 50$ N

2 A car has a resultant driving force of 6000 N and a mass of 1200 kg. Calculate the car's initial acceleration.

Write down the formula in terms of a:	$a = \dfrac{F}{m}$
Substitute the values for F and m:	$a = \dfrac{6000}{1200}$
Work out the answer and write down the units:	$a = 5$ m/s^2

Mass and weight

Scientists use the words 'mass' and 'weight' with special meanings. By the 'mass' of an object we mean how much material is present in it.

Weight is the force on the object due to gravity. It is measured in **newtons** (N). The weight of an object depends on its **mass** and **gravity**. Any mass near the Earth has weight due to the Earth's gravitational pull.

Weight is calculated using the equation:

weight = mass × gravitational field strength

$W = mg$

Scientists often use the word 'field'. We say that there is a 'gravitational field' around the Earth, and that any object that enters this field will be attracted to the Earth.

The value of the gravitational field strength on Earth is 9.8 N/kg, though we usually round it up to 10 N/kg to make the calculations easier. A force of 10 N is needed to lift a 1 kg mass on Earth.

Note that gravity does not stop suddenly as you leave the Earth. Satellites go round the Earth and do not escape because the Earth is still pulling them, even if less strongly than before the satellites were launched. The Earth is even pulling the Moon gently, and this is why it orbits the Earth once per month. And the Earth goes round the Sun because the Sun's gravity is pulling the Earth.

If you stand on the Moon you will feel the gravity of the Moon pulling you down. Your mass will be the same as on Earth, but your weight will be less. This is because the gravity on the Moon is about one-sixth of that on the Earth, and so the force of attraction of an object to the Moon is about one-sixth of that on the Earth. The gravitational field strength on the Moon is 1.6 N/kg, and so a force of 1.6 N is needed to lift a 1 kg mass.

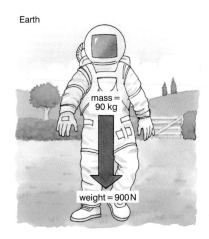
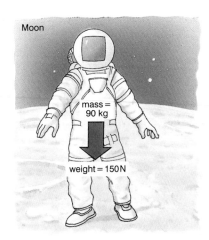

Earth

mass = 90 kg

weight = 900 N

Moon

mass = 90 kg

weight = 150 N

Though your mass remains the same, your weight is greater on Earth than it would be on the Moon.

If two astronauts played football, it would just as difficult to halt a rush by one of them on the Moon as it would be on the Earth, and any collision between them would hurt just as much. The reason is that it is the mass of an object that resists any change in the motion of the object, and the mass of each astronaut is the same in both places.

It is harder to get a massive object moving, and it is harder to stop it once it is moving.

A supertanker laden with oil and travelling at 18 km/h will take over 12 km to stop. A speedboat travelling at the same speed will take less than 100 m. The difference is due to the mass of the tanker.

HOW DO YOU WEIGH SOMETHING?

The balance is level when the forces pulling down both sides are the same. In the balance shown, the forces of 10 N and 20 N on the one side balance the force of 30 N on the other side. The balance compares the weight of the objects on each side. If the balance is on the surface of the Earth, then the masses of these objects are 1 kg and 2 kg on one side, and 3 kg on the other. So the balance also allows you to compare masses.

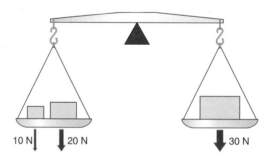

10 N   20 N   30 N

Note that this type of balance would also work on the Moon.

Falling objects and terminal velocity

As a skydiver jumps from a plane, the force of gravity will be much greater than the opposing force caused by air resistance. Initially she will accelerate downwards at 10 m/s^2.

The skydiver's speed will increase rapidly – and the force caused by the air resistance increases as the skydiver's speed increases. Eventually it will exactly match the force of gravity, the forces will be balanced and the speed of the skydiver will remain constant. This speed is known as the **terminal speed**, typically 180 km/h.

If the skydiver makes herself streamlined by going headfirst, with her arms by her side, then she will cut through the air more easily, and the air resistance force will go down. She will then accelerate again, until the force of air resistance increases again to equal her weight. She will now be going at almost 300 km/h.

A parachute has a very large surface, and produces a very large resistive force, so the terminal speed of a parachutist is quite low. This means that he or she can land relatively safely.

Vehicle stopping distances

When a car driver has to brake, it takes time for him or her to react. During this time the car will be travelling at its normal speed. The distance it travels in this time is called the **thinking distance**.

The driver then puts on the brakes. The distance the car travels while it is braking is called the **braking distance**. The overall **stopping distance** is made up from the thinking distance and the braking distance.

The thinking distance can vary from person to person and from situation to situation. The braking distance can vary from car to car.

Factors affecting thinking distance are:
• speed
• tiredness
• alcohol
• medication, drugs
• level of concentration and distraction.

Factors affecting braking distance are:
• speed
• condition of tyres (amount of tread)
• condition of brakes
• road conditions (dry, wet, icy, gravel, etc.)
• mass of the car.

The parachutist descends slowly, with the air resistance on the parachute causing it to pull upwards with a force exactly equalling the parachutist's weight.

A* EXTRA

• Make sure you think carefully about the *two* opposing forces that lead to terminal velocity. The force causing the motion (e.g. gravity or the force from a car engine) usually remains constant. It is the drag force (e.g. air or water resistance) that increases as the velocity increases, until the two are balanced and the velocity stays constant.

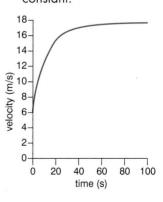

Turning effect of a force

If you have used a spanner to tighten a nut, or you have turned the handle of a rotary beater, you have used a force to turn something. But turning applies to less obvious examples, such as when you push the door handle to close a door, or when a child sits on the end of a see-saw to push her end of it down.

The turning effect of a force is called the **moment** of the force.

The moment of a force depends on two things:
- the size of the force
- the distance between the line of the force and the turning point, which is called the **pivot**.

We calculate the moment of force using this formula:

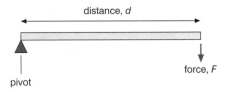

moment of a force = force × distance from pivot

moment = Fd

Moment is measured in newton metres (N m).

F = force in newtons (N)
d = distance in metres (m)

WORKED EXAMPLE
Michelle pushes open a door with a force of 20 N. The door is 0.8 m wide. Calculate the moment of this force.

Write down the formula:	moment = force × distance from pivot
Substitute the values for F and d:	moment = 20 N × 0.8 m
Work out the answer and write down the units:	moment = 16 N m

Centre of mass

The centre of mass is the point where we can assume *all* the mass of the object is concentrated. This is a useful simplification because we can pretend gravity only acts at a single point in the object, so a single arrow on a diagram can represent the weight of an object. For this reason, the centre of mass is sometimes called the **centre of gravity**.

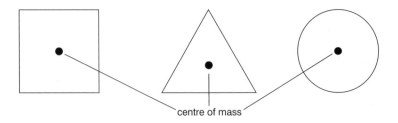

centre of mass

The centre of mass for objects with a regular shape is in the centre.

WHAT ABOUT IRREGULAR SHAPES?

To find the centre of mass of simple objects, such as a piece of card, follow these steps:

1　Hang up the object.
2　Suspend a mass from the same place.
3　Mark the position of the thread.
4　The centre of mass is somewhere along the line of the thread.
5　Repeat steps 1 to 3 with the object suspended from a different place.
6　The centre of mass is where the two lines meet.

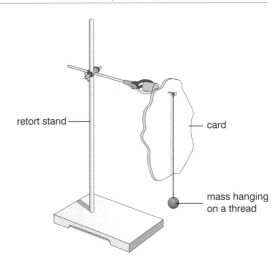

retort stand — card

mass hanging on a thread

CENTRE OF MASS AND STABILITY

The idea of centre of mass is useful when predicting whether or not an object will fall over – whether or not it is **stable**.

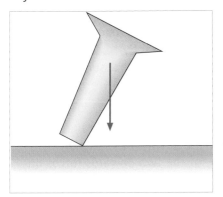

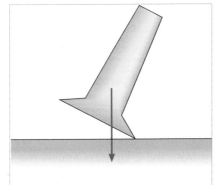

This object will topple over – the centre of mass is outside the pivot so the weight of the object tips it over the rest of the way. The moment of the force turns the object over. An object that is easy to topple is said to be in unstable equilibrium.

This object will fall back into place – the centre of mass is inside the pivot so the weight of the object pulls it back onto its base. The moment of the force returns the object to its base. An object that is difficult to topple is said to be in stable equilibrium.

Principle of moments

If an object is not turning, **the sum of the clockwise moments equals the sum of the anticlockwise moments**. This is the **principle of moments**.

WORKED EXAMPLE
Phil and Jenny are sitting on a see-saw.
The see-saw is balanced on a pivot.
Work out Phil's weight.

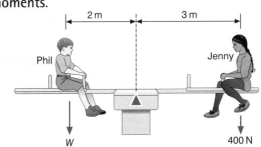

2 m　　3 m

Phil　　Jenny

W　　400 N

Forces on the see-saw

Jenny is causing the clockwise moment of 400 N × 3 m.

Phil is causing the anticlockwise moment of W × 2 m.

The see-saw is balanced, so

the sum of the clockwise moments = the sum of the anticlockwise moments

$$400 \times 3 = W \times 2$$

$$W = 600 \text{ N}$$

A* EXTRA

- Questions involving balancing can look quite difficult. Work out each moment in turn and add together the moments that turn in the same direction.

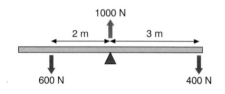

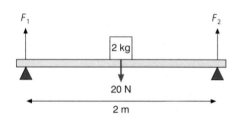

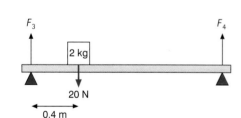

CONDITIONS FOR EQUILIBRIUM

We use the word 'system' to describe a collection of objects working together. So in the example of the see-saw, the two children and the see-saw form a system. We say that a system is in equilibrium if it is not moving in any direction and it is *not* rotating. We already know that for a system not to be moving, the forces on it must be equal and opposite. So:

> For a system to be in equilibrium, there must be no resultant force and no resultant turning effect.

In the case of the balanced see-saw , we have already shown that the there is no resultant turning effect on the see-saw because the clockwise and anticlockwise turning effects are equal and opposite. In addition, the downward weight of the two children on the see-saw is 1000 N, and the upward force on the see-saw from the pivot must also be 1000 N.

Forces on a beam

Let us look at the forces on a beam that is supporting a load. Scientists often make some approximations that cannot be exactly true, but which make it easier to understand a situation. In this case, we assume that the beam is light compared with the load it is supporting, and we will ignore its weight completely.

If the beam is in equilibrium and is not moving, then the forces are in balance, and we can immediately say that the downwards force on the beam from the 2 kg mass equals the value of the two upwards forces on the beam from the two supports added together:

$$F_1 + F_2 = 20 \text{ N}$$

(Note that the question is 'What is happening to the beam?' So we are considering the three forces that are trying to move *the beam*. The 2 kg mass is trying to push it downwards, and the two supports are trying to push it upwards. It is perfectly fair to ask questions such as 'Which way is the beam trying to push the 2 kg mass?' but that is *not* the question to ask here!)

If the mass is put in the middle of the beam, then it is obvious that the two forces are equal and that

$$F_1 + F_2 = 10 \text{ N}$$

If the mass is to one end of the beam, then the forces F_3 and F_4 will not be equal. It is still true that $F_3 + F_4 = 20$ N, but how do we calculate the individual values? The easiest way is to note that the beam is not rotating around the left-hand pivot! That immediately tells us that the anticlockwise moment of F_4 about this pivot equals the clockwise moment of the 20 N about the pivot:

$$2 \times F_4 = 0.4 \times 20$$
$$F_4 = (0.4 \times 20) \div 2 = 4 \text{ N}$$

Because $\quad F_3 + F_4 = 20$ N,
$$F_3 = 16 \text{ N}$$

You will want to check that if you start by saying that the beam is not rotating about the right-hand pivot, you still get the same answers for F_3 and F_4.

How are materials affected by stretching?

A music wire string, such as a guitar string, will behave as shown in the graph for wire, but will break shortly after the limit of proportionality is reached.

A piece of rubber stretches a quite a lot for small forces. The long polymer molecules are being 'straightened out'. Once this is done it becomes much stiffer and harder to extend further. However, unless it breaks, its behaviour is elastic.

A copper wire has a large plastic section on the graph. As it stretches, the wire becomes thinner and thinner until it finally breaks. This stretching is irreversible, and the extension is caused by 'plastic flow'.

A strip of polythene will stretch relatively easily, but it will scarcely shorten at all when the load is removed. This means that polythene stretches almost entirely by plastic flow. This was the original meaning of the word 'plastic'. When people started to invent new materials in the early 1900s, many of them stretched in a plastic way. The word was then used to describe them.

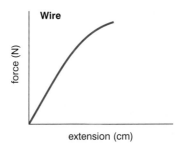

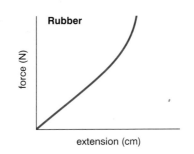

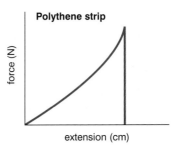

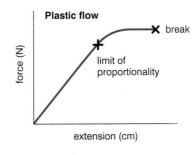

A* EXTRA

- During elastic behaviour, the particles in the material are pulled apart a little. During plastic behaviour the particles slide past each other, and the structure of the material is changed permanently.
  A material shows *elastic* behaviour if it returns to its original length when any deforming forces have been removed. During elastic behaviour, the particles in the material are pulled apart a little, so they return to their original positions when the forces are removed.
  A material shows *plastic* behaviour if it remains deformed when a load is removed. During plastic behaviour the particles slide past each other and the structure of the material is changed permanently.

Force–extension graphs for a metal wire, for rubber, for a polythene strip, and to show plastic flow.

Hooke's law

When a spring stretches, the extension of the spring is proportional to the force stretching it, provided the elastic limit of the spring is not exceeded. This is **Hooke's law** and is shown by a straight line on a graph.

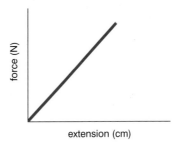

Elastic behaviour in a spring is shown by a straight line.

The gradient of the line is a measure of the stiffness of the spring.

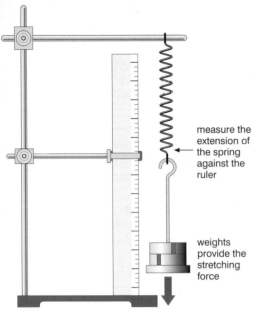

An experiment to measure Hooke's law

1 Assemble the apparatus (left) and allow the spring to hang down. Measure the starting position on the ruler.

2 Take the first mass, which consists of the hook and base plate, typically of mass 100 g (a weight of 1 N), and hang it on the spring. Measure the new position on the ruler. The difference in the readings is the extension of the spring.

3 Add masses one by one to the first one. Typically each mass is C-shaped, and adds an additional 100 g. Add the masses carefully so that the spring stretches slowly.

4 You may want to reverse the experiment to see what happens as the masses are removed.

5 Calculate the extension, and plot a graph of extension against force.

measure the extension of the spring against the ruler

weights provide the stretching force

Mass (g)	Force (N)	Reading (cm)	Calculate the extension (cm)	Extension (cm)
0	0	15.2	–	–
100	1.0	16.8	16.8 – 15.2	1.6
200	2.0	18.5	18.5 – 15.2	3.3
300	3.0	19.9	19.9 – 15.2	4.7
400	4.0	21.6	21.6 – 15.2	6.4
etc	etc			

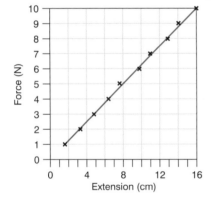

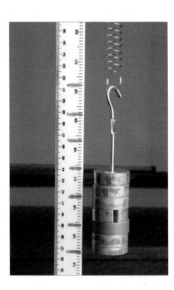

A spring that obeys Hooke's law shows 'proportional' behaviour: the extension of the spring increases in proportion to the load on the spring. It also shows **elastic** behaviour – when the force is removed, the spring returns to its original length.

LIMIT OF PROPORTIONALITY

If you stretch the spring too far, the line is no longer straight, and Hooke's law is no longer true. This point at the end of the straight line is know as the 'limit of proportionality'.

The spring may (if you do not stretch it too far) be elastic and go back to its original length.

But as you stretch the material beyond the limit of proportionality, different materials can behave in widely different ways.

The equation for Hooke's law is:

force = spring constant × extension of spring	F = force in newtons
$F = kx$	k = spring constant in N/m
	x = extension of the spring in m

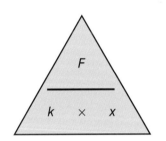

Note that it is acceptable to use a spring constant in N/cm or N/mm, so long as the extension is measured in the same units.

This equation works for springs that are being stretched or compressed. The value of k will be the same for both, but note that some springs cannot be compressed (if, for example, the turns of the spring are already in contact).

WORKED EXAMPLE

A motorbike has a single compression spring on the rear wheels. When the cyclist sits on the bike, she pushes on the rear wheel with 60 per cent of her weight. If her mass is 50 kg, and the spring constant is 60 N/cm, how much does the spring compress when she sits on the bike?

Write down the formula for the weight of the cyclist: $W = mg$
Substitue the values for m and g: $W = 50 \times 10$
Work out the answer and write down the units: $W = 500$ N

The force on the rear spring $= 60$ per cent of 500 N
$= 0.6 \times 500$ N
$= 300$ N

Write down the formula for the compression of the spring: $x = \dfrac{F}{k}$

Substitute the values for F and k: $x = \dfrac{300}{60}$

Work out the answer and write down the units: $x = 5$ cm

The spring compresses by 5 cm.

REVIEW QUESTIONS

Note that the gravitational field strength on the surface of Mars is 3.8 N/kg.

Q1 A teenage astronaut has a mass of 60 kg when she gets into her spacecraft on Earth.
  a What is her weight on Earth?
  Parts b–e refer to the situation on the surface of Mars.
  b What is her mass now?
  c What is her weight now?
  d If she stands in one pan of a large balance, what masses would be needed in the other pan to balance her?
  e If she stands on bathroom scales (which are a type of spring balance) what would be the reading in newtons?

Q2 The height that you can jump depends inversely on the gravitational field strength. So if the field strength doubles, the height halves. If the Olympic Games were held on Mars in a large dome to provide air to breathe, what would happen to the records for:
  a weight lifting (weight in N)
  b high jump (height)
  c pole vault (height)
  d throwing the javelin (distance)
  e the 100 m race (time)?
  In every case, describe what is likely to happen to the record, choosing between:
  (i) increase   (ii) stay similar   (iii) decrease
  and explain your choice.

Q3 The diagram shows the stages in the descent of a skydiver.
  a Describe and explain the motion of the skydiver in each case.
  b In stage 5 explain why the parachutist does not sink into the ground.

Q4 Terry performed an experiment stretching a spring. She loaded masses onto the spring and measured its extension. Here are her results.

Extension in cm	0	4	8	12	16	20	24
Load in N	0	2.0	4.0	6.0	7.5	8.3	8.6

  a On graph paper, plot a graph of load (vertical axis) against extension (horizontal axis).
  Draw a suitable line through your points.
  b Mark on the graph the limit of proportionality, and indicate the region where proportional behaviour occurs and the region where the behaviour is probably plastic.
  c How does Terry check whether the spring, after being loaded with 8.6 N, has shown plastic behaviour or purely elastic behaviour?

1   600 N

2   600 N
     600 N

     1000 N

3   600 N

     600 N

4   600 N

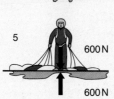

5   600 N

     600 N

Q5 The manufacturer of a car gave the following information:
Mass of car 1000 kg. The car will accelerate from 0 to 30 m/s in 12 seconds.

　a Calculate the average acceleration of the car during the 12 seconds.

　b Calculate the force needed to produce this acceleration.

Q6 Two tug boats have ropes attached to a ship and are about to start moving it very carefully. One tug is north of the ship and is pulling with a force of 3000 N, and the other tug is east of the ship and is pulling with a force of 4000 N.

　a By means of a diagram calculate the total force with which the ship will be pulled, and show the direction in which it will be pulled.

　b The ship has a mass of 500 tonnes (1 tonne = 1000 kg).

　　(i)　Calculate the acceleration of the ship.

　　(ii)　Calculate the speed of the ship after 10 s.

Q7 A flag is being blown by the wind. The force on the flag is 100 N and the flagpole is 8 m tall.
Calculate the moment of the force about the base of the flagpole.

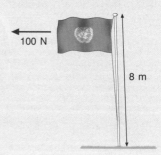

100 N

8 m

Q8 Which of these glasses is the most stable? Explain your answer.

A　　　B　　　C

Q9 Rod and Jane are sitting on a see-saw. The see-saw is not balanced. Freddy weighs 300 N. Where should Freddy sit in order to balance the see-saw?

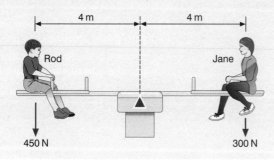

4 m　　　4 m

Rod　　　Jane

450 N　　　300 N

More questions on the CD ROM

Three-cylinder engine with just sufficient power for cruise and battery

Valve drive mechanism with adjustable timing

Fuel injection system designed to allow extremely lean fuel mixtures

Inlet valve

Exhaust valve

Ultra-low friction piston with cut-away skirt

Motor-generator with the following functions:

- High speed starter motor for instant starts (motor is always turned off instead of being allowed to idle)
- Electric motor to assist the engine when the driver wishes to accelerate
- Alternator to charge battery and provide electricity for lights, power steering etc.
- Regenerative brake to slow car by turning kinetic energy into stored electrical energy in the battery

Cars of tomorrow

So is the electric car the solution for the future? These cars aim to be more fuel efficient, so that you can travel further while using the same amount of petrol. Certainly they are an improvement, but they may not be the final solution. The efficient use of electricity and electrical circuits in vehicles is an area where there is much to find out and more development to be done. Spend a little time on your own research and see what you can find out.

ELECTRICITY

MAINS ELECTRICITY

Electricity is a clean and effective method of generating heat and movement in many situations in the home. When the appliance in the home is switched on, a circuit is completed between the local substation and the appliance. Electricity is forced to flow along the 'live' wire from the substation, through the appliance, and back along the 'neutral' wire to the substation. Here it is 'pumped' back to the house again. Some appliances have a third wire, the 'earth' wire. You will also meet the American word 'ground' instead of 'earth'. This wire does not normally carry any current, but it is there for safety, as discussed below.

Electrical hazards

Electricity can cause hazards in domestic situations. For example:

Hazard	Danger
Frayed cables	Wiring can become exposed
Long cables	These might cause a trip or a fall
Damaged plugs	Wiring can become exposed
Water around sockets	Water conducts, so can connect a person into the mains supply
Pushing metal objects into sockets	This connects the holder to the mains supply

If there is a fault in an electrical appliance, it could take too much electrical current. This might make the appliance itself dangerous, or it could cause the flex between the appliance and the wall to become too hot and start a fire.

Insulation, fuses and circuit breakers

The laws for the safe use of electricity are constantly being refined by governments, and an electrician will need to learn to work to the latest safety standards. The most important aids to the safe use of electricity are insulation and fuses or circuit breakers.

Insulation these days is generally a plastic such as PVC, used to cover the copper wires and prevent them from touching each other, and to prevent the operator from touching them. In areas that will go above 100°C, other plastics, glass or ceramic are used.

The electric current usually has to pass through a **fuse** or **circuit breaker** before it reaches the appliance. If there is a sudden surge in the current, the wire in the fuse will heat up and melt – it 'blows'. This breaks the circuit and stops any further current flowing. If a circuit breaker is used, then the circuit breaker springs open (trips) a switch if there is an increase in current in the circuit. This can be reset easily after the fault in the circuit has been corrected.

In all houses there will be a distribution box that takes all of the electricity for the house and sends it to the different rooms. In old houses this box may still use fuses, but in modern installations, the box will use miniature circuit breakers, often known as MCBs.

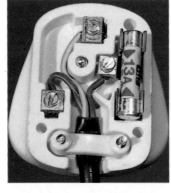

In some countries the fuse is fitted into the plug of the appliance. The fuse fits between the live brown wire and the pin. The brown live wire and the blue neutral wire carry the current. The green and yellow striped earth wire is needed to make metal appliances safer.

Where a fuse is fitted to the plug, it must have a value above the normal current that the appliance needs but should be as small as possible. For fuses in the plug, the most common fuses are rated at 3 A, 5 A and 13 A. Any electrical appliance with a heating element in it should be fitted with at least a 13 A fuse.

Metal-cased appliances must have an **earth wire** as well as a fuse. If the live wire worked loose and came into contact with the metal casing, the casing would become live and the user could be electrocuted. The earth wire provides a very low resistance route to the 0 V earth – usually water pipes buried deep underground. This low resistance means that a large current passes from the live wire to earth, causing the fuse to melt and break the circuit. Note that the appliance will be extremely dangerous, but will appear to work correctly, if the earth wire is not fitted correctly or if it has broken. If there is any doubt about the earthing of the appliance, or indeed of the whole house, it must be checked by an electrician.

Appliances that are made with plastic casing do not need an earth wire. The plastic is an insulator and so can never become live. Appliances like this are said to be **double insulated**.

In situations that may expose people to electricity unexpectedly (for example using an electric drill, especially drilling into a wall with hidden power cables, or using power tools out of doors, perhaps in wet conditions), a residual current circuit breaker (RCCB) must be used in the power socket on the wall. If any of the electricity starts to leak out, the RCCB will turn off the power in 30 ms or less. The RCCB cannot be guaranteed to save the user's life, but it gives them a much better chance of surviving the accident.

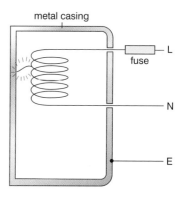

The earth wire and fuse work together to make sure that the metal outer casing of this appliance can never become live and electrocute someone.

Electrical heating and current in a resistor

Many household appliances consist of an electrically heated resistor. You only need to think of the electric kettle, the electric fire, light bulb, domestic iron, electric oven. Even the washing machine, the dishwasher, the tumble drier and the hairdryer consist of an electric heater with an electric motor added.

If you touch the electric flex to one of the above electric heaters when it is switched on, you will notice that the flex is either at room temperature or, perhaps, it will be slightly warm to the touch. The electric current is increasing the temperature of the heater, by giving it energy, but it is not having the same effect on the flex.

The reason is that the heater has a higher **resistance**, to make it difficult for the electricity to flow through it. The flex contains copper wires to feed the electricity to and from the heater. Copper has a very low resistance – only silver has lower, and silver is seldom used for the obvious reason of high cost!

So when an electric current passes through a resistor, energy that was originally created in the power station, where it was converted into electrical energy, is converted into internal energy in the heater, and its temperature increases.

Note that if two heaters are each connected to the mains power, it is the one with the lower resistance that will allow more current to flow, and will become the hotter. This is why it is so important that the live wire and the neutral wire in the flex do not touch. If they do touch, they make a very low resistance circuit, and the flex would burst into flames if the correct fuse is not fitted to break the circuit.

Power, current and voltage

The **voltage** ('pressure') with which the power station tries to drive electricity through the household appliances is measured in **volts** (V). The voltage between the live socket and the neutral socket on the wall varies from region to region. The most common options are 230 V and 120 V, though there are many other standards such as 200 V, 127 V and 100 V. Some equipment can adapt to run on any voltage, but some will be destroyed if it is connected to the wrong voltage, especially if it is too high.

All electrical equipment has a **power rating**, which indicates how many joules of energy are supplied each second. The unit of power used is the **watt** (W). Light bulbs often have power ratings of 60 W or 100 W. Electric kettles have ratings of about 2 kilowatts (2 kW = 2000 W). A 2 kW kettle supplies 2000 J of energy each second.

The power of a piece of electrical equipment depends on the voltage and the current:

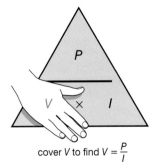

cover V to find $V = \dfrac{P}{I}$

power = voltage × current

P = power in watts (W)
I = current in amps (A)
V = voltage in volts (V)

WORKED EXAMPLES

1   What is the power of an electric toaster if a current of 7 A is obtained from a 230 V supply?

Write down the formula in terms of P:	$P = V \times I$
Substitute the values:	$P = 230 \times 7$
Work out the answer and write down the unit:	$P = 1610\,W$

2   An electric oven has a power rating of 2 kW. What current will flow when the oven is used with a 230 V supply?

Write down the formula in terms of I:	$I = \dfrac{P}{V}$
Substitute the values:	$I = \dfrac{2000}{230}$
Work out the answer and write down the unit:	$I = 8.7\,A$

3   What fuse should be fitted in the plug of a 2.2 kW electric kettle used with a supply voltage of 230 V?

Calculate the normal current:	$I = \dfrac{P}{V}$
	$= \dfrac{2200\,W}{230\,V}$
	$= 9.6\,A$

Choose the fuse with the smallest rating bigger than the normal current: the fuse must be 13 A (3 A, 5 A and 13 A fuses are available).

4   What fuse should be fitted to the plug of a reading lamp which has a 60 W lamp and a supply of 230 V?

Calculate the normal current:	$I = \dfrac{P}{V}$
	$= \dfrac{60\,\text{W}}{230\,\text{V}}$
	$= 0.26\,\text{A}$

Choose the fuse with the smallest rating bigger than the normal current: the fuse must be 3 A.

Energy, current, voltage and time

If you switch on an electric kettle for a minute or a room heater for five minutes, then you can measure the temperature increase of the water in the kettle or of the room. The temperature will increase because energy has been given to the water or to the room. Energy is measured in **joules** (J). A heater rated at 1 watt will give out 1 joule of heat each second. A 2 kW heater will give out 2000 joules per second, and if the heater is switched on for 4 s, it will give out 8000 J.

energy = current × voltage × time

$E = I \times V \times t$

E = the energy transferred in joules (J)

I = current in amperes (A)

V = voltage in volts (V)

t = time in seconds (s)

WORKED EXAMPLE

Calculate the energy transferred when a 12 V motor, running at a current of 0.5 A, is left on for 5 minutes.

Write down the formula:	$E = I \times V \times t$
Substitute the values: (remember the time *must* be in seconds)	$E = 0.5 \times 12 \times 300$
Work out the answer and write down the unit:	$E = 1800\,\text{J}$

Alternating current and direct current

A battery produces a steady current. The electrons are constantly flowing from the negative terminal of the battery round the circuit and back to the positive terminal. This produces a **direct current** (d.c.).

The mains electricity used in the home is quite different. The electrons in the circuit move backwards and forwards. This kind of current is called **alternating current** (a.c.). Mains electricity moves forwards and backwards 50 times each second, that is, with a frequency of 50 hertz (Hz). The frequency chosen varies from country to country.

The advantage of using an a.c. source of electricity rather than a d.c. source is that it can be transmitted from power stations to the home at very high voltages, which reduces the amount of energy that is lost in the overhead cables.

REVIEW QUESTIONS

Q1 **a** A hairdryer works on mains electricity of 230 V and takes a current of 4 A. Calculate the power of the hairdryer.

b In some countries it is illegal to have power sockets in a bathroom, to stop you using hairdryers. Why would it be foolish to use a hairdryer near to a washbasin?

Q2 In her living room, Felicity has the following items:
- three 100 W lamps
- a TV that takes 2 A
- a hi-fi audio system that takes 1 A
- a 2 kW electric heater
- a 3 kW air conditioning unit.

The whole room is supplied from a 220 V a.c. power supply through one miniature circuit breaker (MCB). What rating of MCB should you fit, if values of 10 A, 20 A, 30 A, 40 A, 50 A and 60 A are available? How would your answer change if the supply were 120 V a.c.?

More questions on the CD ROM

ENERGY AND POTENTIAL DIFFERENCE IN CIRCUITS

Videos & questions on the CD ROM

When people started using electricity, they quickly found that it was not convenient to draw accurate pictures of the circuits that they made. It was much easier to understand how the circuit worked, and to correct faults, if they used standard symbols for the parts. It was also much easier if the wires were drawn in straight lines, rather than trying to copy the exact route taken.

Study the circuits used in this chapter and learn the symbols and what they represent.

This simple circuit shows how a flashlight is powered by a **battery** consisting of three 1.5 V **cells**, giving a total of 4.5 V. In the case of a flashlight, the cells are put in separately, but in the case of a 9 V battery, for example, the six cells are pre-assembled by the manufacturer. The word 'battery' means an assembly of several cells, but people often use the word to refer to a single cell.

The '+' terminal of the cell is indicated by the long thin line, and the '-' terminal by the short thick line. It may help you to remember this if you imagine yourself cutting the long thin line into two shorter pieces and turning them into a + sign.

The other symbols in the circuit are the **normally open switch**, and the **lamp**.

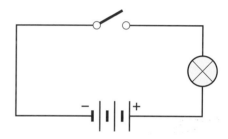

A circuit for a flashlight

Series and parallel circuits

If you want to power two or more lights or heaters from a.c. or from a d.c. battery, you can place them in series or in parallel.

If they are in **series**, then exactly the same electric current flows through each of the components in the circuit. The voltage is shared between the units in the circuit. Thus it is possible to join in series two identical lamps designed for 6 V and then to connect them to a 12 V battery.

In a **parallel** circuit, the current splits and part of it goes through each component in the circuit. All of the appliances in a house are connected in parallel to the mains supply, and each one sees the full 120 V or 230 V of the mains supply when it is switched on. The two overwhelming advantages of the parallel arrangement are that each appliance can be designed to work with the mains voltage supply, and that the appliances can be switched on and off individually.

All of these lights are in parallel. If they were in series then they would all go off if any one of them was switched off.

There are two different ways of connecting two lamps to the same battery. Two very different kinds of circuit can be made. These circuits are called **series** and **parallel** circuits.

	Series	Parallel
Circuit diagram		
Appearance of the lamps	Both lamps have the same brightness, both lamps are dim.	Both lamps have the same brightness, both lamps are bright.
Battery	The battery is having a hard time pushing the same charge first through one bulb, then another. This means less charge flows each second, so there is a low current and energy is slowly transferred from the battery.	The battery pushes the charge along two alternative paths. This means more charge can flow around the circuit each second, so energy is quickly transferred from the battery.
Switches	The lamps cannot be switched on and off independently.	The lamps can be switched on and off independently by putting switches in the parallel branches.
Advantages/ disadvantages	A very simple circuit to make. The battery will last longer. If one lamp 'blows' then the circuit is broken so the other one goes out too.	The battery will not last as long. If one lamp 'blows' the other one will keep working.
Examples	Christmas tree lights are often connected in series.	Electric lights in the home are connected in parallel.

Current in a series circuit

The current flowing in a circuit can be measured using an **ammeter**. If you want to measure the current flowing through a particular component, such as a lamp or motor, the ammeter must be connected **in series** with the component. In a series circuit, the current is the same no matter where the ammeter is put. This is not the case with a parallel circuit.

The voltage across a component can be measured using a voltmeter, as shown in the diagram below right.

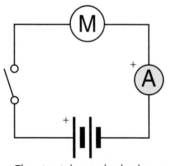

The circuit has to be broken to include the ammeter.

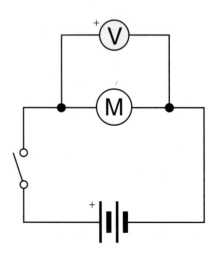

The voltmeter can be added after the circuit has been made.

In a series circuit, the current that flows round the circuit depends on the applied voltage and on the number and the nature of the components in the circuit. For example, it is possible to buy strings of lights designed to decorate trees. Some of these use lamps that are designed to be connected to 12 V and to pass 1 A of current. So the lamps are 12 W each. If the string of lights connects 20 of these in series for connection to a 240 V supply, then each lamp will have 12 V across it, and the current through the string will be 1 A, with exactly the same current going through each lamp.

If any one lamp is removed or breaks, all of the lamps will go off. Treat this string with great care if you are trying to check which lamp is faulty. The lamps may only be 12 V, but when you remove the faulty bulb, the voltage on one contact inside the socket will be 240 V!

If the lamps are connected to a lower voltage, such as a 120 V supply, then the current will be approximately half of this through each lamp, and the lamps will glow very dimly.

If the components in the series circuit are not identical, then the current through each one will still be exactly the same, but those with a higher resistance to the flow of electricity will use up more of the supply voltage, and those with a lower resistance will use up less; but the total voltage across all of the components together will be the supply voltage, of course.

How current varies with voltage

To measure how current varies with voltage, we use this circuit (right). The component (lamp, resistor or whatever) is placed in a circuit with an ammeter to measure the current through the component, and with a voltmeter to measure the voltage across it. To power the circuit you could use a battery as shown, or you could use a power supply with a suitable output. To take readings, the circuit is switched on, and readings are made of the voltage and the current.

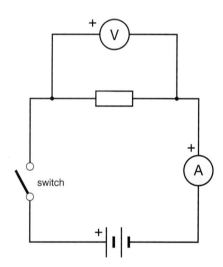

You can then plot a graph of voltage against current.

Note that the readings may change a little over the first few seconds. If so, this is probably because the component is heating up and its resistance is changing. If this happens, you would have to decide whether to take the readings before the component has heated up, and so measure the resistance at room temperature, or to wait until the readings have stopped changing. This would give you the 'steady-state' resistance with the component at its usual running temperature.

You may wish to change the voltage of the battery by changing the number of cells (or you may adjust the output of the power supply).

For components like **resistors** and **thin wires**, the current through the component doubles if you double the voltage, triples if you triple the voltage, etc. The resistance of the component to the passage of electricity does not change, and the extra current is caused solely by the increased pressure of the extra voltage. The current is directly proportional to the voltage, and the graph is a straight line.

Take care! If you try **thick wire**, the current will be extremely high for a very low voltage. The wire can get very hot very quickly and there is a risk of injury.

The resistance of most conductors becomes higher if the temperature of the conductor increases. As the temperature rises, the particles in the conductor vibrate more and provide greater resistance to the flow of electrons. For example, the resistance of a filament lamp becomes greater as the voltage is increased and the lamp gets hotter.

In an 'ohmic' resistor, such as carbon (left-hand graph), Ohm's law applies and the voltage is directly proportional to the current – a straight line is obtained. In a filament lamp (right-hand graph), Ohm's law is not obeyed because the heating of the lamp changes its resistance.

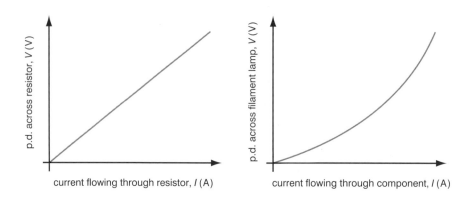

It does not matter which way the current flows through a lamp, but a pocket calculator, say, could be destroyed if the battery is not inserted correctly. One way to prevent this is to add a **diode** to the circuit.

In this circuit the calculator is represented as a resistor. A calculator is far more complicated than that, but it does behave to the battery *as if* it were a resistor, drawing a small current *I* out of the battery.

As you can see, the arrow on the diode shows the way that conventional current can flow. When the battery is inserted the wrong way round, no current can flow.

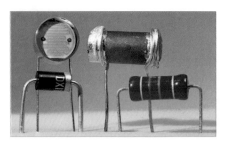

A light-dependent resistor, (top left) conducts better when light shines on it. A thermistor (top right) conducts better when it is hot. A diode (bottom left) only conducts in one direction. An ordinary (ohmic) resistor is shown bottom right.

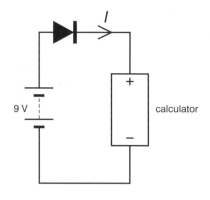

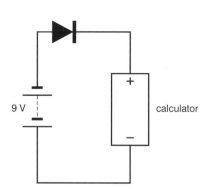

Effect on current of changing resistance

As we have noted, using more voltage across a component will increase the current through it. The amount of current flowing through a circuit can also be controlled by changing the resistance of the circuit using a variable resistor or rheostat. Adjustment of the rheostat changes the length of the wire the current has to flow through. Variable resistors are often used, for example, to change the brightness of the lighting in a car.

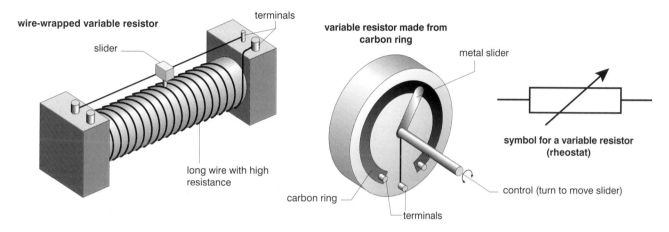

Variable resistors are commonly used in electrical equipment, for example in the speed controls of model racing cars or in volume controls on radios and hi-fi systems.

The thermistor and the LDR

In some substances, increasing the temperature actually **lowers** the resistance. This is the case with **semiconductors** such as silicon. Silicon has few free electrons and so behaves more like an insulator than a conductor. But if silicon is heated, more electrons are removed from the outer electron shells of the atoms producing an increased electron cloud. The released electrons can move throughout the structure, allowing an electric current to move more easily. This effect is large enough to outweigh the increase in resistance that might be expected from the increased vibration of the silicon ions in the structure as the temperature increases.

Semiconducting silicon is used to make **thermistors**, which are used as temperature sensors, and **light-dependent resistors** (LDRs), which are used as light sensors.

In LDRs it is light energy that removes electrons from the silicon atoms, increasing the electron cloud. So LDRs have a very high resistance in the dark, and a very low resistance in the light. LDRs are used in street lamps that switch on automatically at night, and in the type of burglar alarm that sets a light beam (usually an infra-red beam so that it is invisible) across the path of the burglar.

A* EXTRA

- In a thermistor, increasing temperature actually reduces the resistance. This is the opposite effect to that in a normal resistor.
- In a light-dependent resistor (LDR) an increase in brightness reduces the resistance.

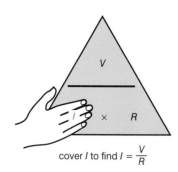

cover *I* to find $I = \frac{V}{R}$

A* EXTRA

- This equation is often called Ohm's law, but it is certainly not a 'law', it's just the definition of the resistance of an object. The idea of resistance is useful because for a lot of objects their resistance does not change when you change the current through them. But there are many components, such as light bulbs, for which this is not true.

Voltage, current and resistance

The relationship between voltage, current and resistance in electrical circuits is given by this equation.

voltage = current × resistance

$V = I \times R$

> *V* is the voltage in volts (V)
>
> *I* is the current in amps (A)
>
> *R* is the resistance in ohms (Ω)

It is important to be able to rearrange this equation when performing calculations. Use the triangle on the right to help you.

WORKED EXAMPLES

1   Calculate the resistance of a heater element if the current is 10 A when it is connected to a 230 V supply.

Write down the formula in terms of *R*:	$R = \frac{V}{I}$
Substitute the values for *V* and *I*:	$R = \frac{230}{10}$
Work out the answer and write down the unit:	$R = 23 \ \Omega$

2   A 6 V supply is applied to 1000 Ω resistor. What current will flow?

Write down the formula in terms of *I*:	$I = \frac{V}{R}$
Substitute the values for *V* and *R*:	$I = \frac{6}{1000}$
Work out the answer and write down the unit:	$I = 0.006 \ A$

Current is the rate of flow of charge

All materials contain electrons, but in many materials they are all 'locked' into the material's atoms and cannot move about. These materials cannot carry an electric current, and are called electrical **insulators**. Materials in which there are large numbers of electrons that are free to move around from atom to atom are called **conductors**.

When there is no current in a conductor, the free electrons move randomly between atoms, with no overall movement. When you connect it in an electrical circuit with a power source like a battery, there is a current in the conductor. Now the electrons drift in one direction, while still moving in a random way as well. The drift speed is very slow, often only a few millimetres each second. A current can only flow in a conductor if it is connected in a complete circuit. If the circuit is broken, the current stops.

The size of an electric current depends on the number of electrons that are moving and how fast they are moving. But instead of measuring the actual number of electrons we use the total charge carried by the electrons round the circuit each second.

Electric current is measured in **amperes**, or **amps** (A).

If one amp of current is flowing down a wire, then one coulomb of charge is passing any point on the circuit each second. (1 A = 1 C/s.)

You use an ammeter to measure current in an electrical circuit. If the current is very small, you might use a milliammeter, which measures current in milliamps (1 mA = 0.001 A). Even smaller currents are measured with a microammeter.

If you want to measure the current flowing through a particular component, such as a lamp or motor, the ammeter must be connected **in series** with the component. In a series circuit, the current is the same no matter where the ammeter is put. This is not the case with a parallel circuit.

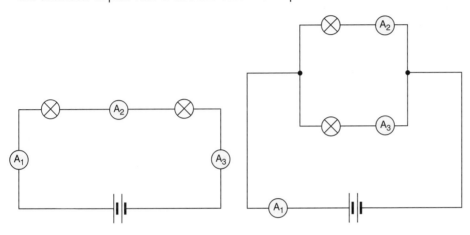

A* EXTRA

• The current is the same in all parts of a series circuit but the potential difference across different components can be different.

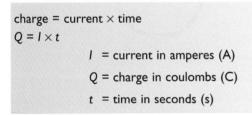

In this series circuit, the current will be the same throughout the circuit so $A_1 = A_2 = A_3$.

The current flow splits between the two branches of the parallel circuit so $A_1 = A_2 + A_3$.

The electric current is the amount of charge flowing every second – the number of coulombs per second:

charge = current × time

$Q = I \times t$

I = current in amperes (A)

Q = charge in coulombs (C)

t = time in seconds (s)

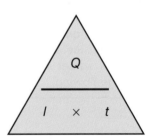

Current in metallic conductors

Scientists now know that electric current is really a **flow of electrons** around the circuit from negative to positive. Unfortunately, early scientists guessed the direction of flow incorrectly. Consequently all diagrams were drawn showing the current flowing from positive to negative. This way of showing the current has not been changed and so the **conventional current** that everyone uses gives the direction that positive charges would flow.

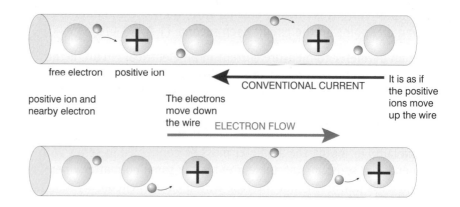

Conventional current is drawn in the opposite direction to electron flow.

free electron   positive ion

positive ion and nearby electron

CONVENTIONAL CURRENT

It is as if the positive ions move up the wire

The electrons move down the wire   ELECTRON FLOW

Voltage, energy and charge

The electrons flowing round a circuit have some potential energy, which can be referred to as electrical energy. As the electrons pass through the battery, or other power supply, they are given potential energy, and as they move around the circuit they transfer the energy to the various components in the circuit. For example, when the electrons move through a lamp they transfer some of their energy to the lamp.

The amount of energy that a unit of charge (a coulomb) transfers between one point and another (the number of joules per coulomb) is called the **potential difference** (p.d.). Potential difference is measured in **volts** and so it is often referred to as **voltage**.

If the potential difference across a lamp, say, is 1 volt, then each coulomb of electricity that passes through the lamp will transfer 1 joule of energy to the lamp.

A* EXTRA

• The potential difference is measured between two points in a circuit. It is like an electrical pressure difference and measures the energy transferred per unit of charge flowing.

Potential difference (p.d.) is the difference in energy of a coulomb of charge between two parts of a circuit.

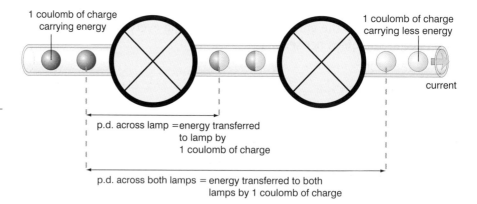

1 coulomb of charge carrying energy

1 coulomb of charge carrying less energy

current

p.d. across lamp = energy transferred to lamp by 1 coulomb of charge

p.d. across both lamps = energy transferred to both lamps by 1 coulomb of charge

MEASURING ELECTRICITY

Potential difference is measured using a **voltmeter**. If you want to measure the p.d. across a component then the voltmeter must be connected across that component. Testing with a voltmeter does not interfere with the circuit.

A voltmeter can be used to show how the potential difference varies in different parts of a circuit. In a series circuit you find different values of the voltage depending on where you attach the voltmeter. You can assume that energy is only transferred when the current passes through electrical components such as lamps and motors – the energy transfer as the current flows through copper connecting wire is very small. It is only possible therefore to measure a p.d. or voltage across a component.

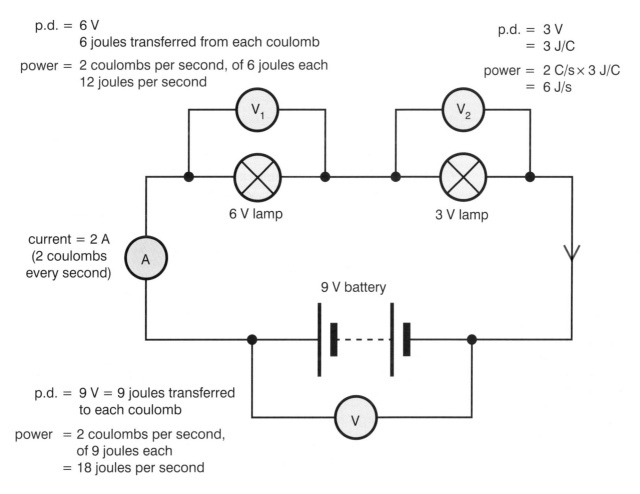

p.d. = 6 V
6 joules transferred from each coulomb

power = 2 coulombs per second, of 6 joules each
12 joules per second

p.d. = 3 V
    = 3 J/C

power = 2 C/s × 3 J/C
    = 6 J/s

V_1

V_2

6 V lamp

3 V lamp

current = 2 A
(2 coulombs
every second)

A

9 V battery

p.d. = 9 V = 9 joules transferred
    to each coulomb

power = 2 coulombs per second,
    of 9 joules each
    = 18 joules per second

V

The potential difference across the battery equals the sum of the potential differences across each lamp. That is $V = V_1 + V_2$.

REVIEW QUESTIONS

Q1 Look at the following circuit diagrams. They show a number of ammeters and in some cases the readings on these ammeters. All the lamps are identical.

a For circuit X, what readings would you expect on ammeters A_1 and A_2?

b For circuit Y, what readings would you expect on ammeters A_4 and A_5?

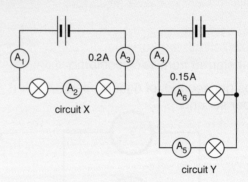

circuit X

circuit Y

Q2 Look at the circuit diagram. It shows how three voltmeters have been added to the circuit. What reading would you expect on V_1?

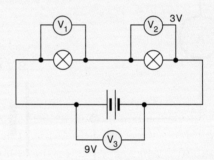

Q3 a A charge of 10 coulombs flows through a motor in 30 seconds. What is the current flowing through the motor?

b A heater uses a current of 10 A. How much charge flows through the lamp in:

i 1 second, ii 1 hour?

Q4 Use Ohm's law to calculate the following:

a The voltage required to produce a current of 2 A in a 12 Ω resistor.

b The voltage required to produce a current of 0.1 A in a 200 Ω resistor.

c The current produced when a voltage of 12 V is applied to a 100 Ω resistor.

d The current produced when a voltage of 230 V is applied to a 10 Ω resistor.

e The resistance of a wire which under a potential difference of 6 V allows a current of 0.1 A to flow.

f The resistance of a heater which under a potential difference of 230 V allows a current of 10 A to flow.

More questions on the CD ROM

ELECTRIC CHARGE

Videos & questions on the CD ROM

Conductors and insulators

Substances that allow an electric current to flow through them are called **conductors**; those which do not are called **insulators**.

Metals are conductors. In a metal structure, the metal atoms exist as ions surrounded by an electron cloud. If a potential difference is applied to the metal, the electrons in this cloud are able to move and a current flows.

When the electrons are moving through the metal structure, they bump into the metal ions and this causes **resistance** to the electron flow or current. In different conductors the ease of flow of the electrons is different and so the conductors have different resistances. For instance, copper is a better conductor than iron.

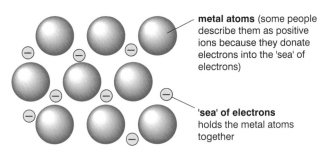

metal atoms (some people describe them as positive ions because they donate electrons into the 'sea' of electrons)

'sea' of electrons holds the metal atoms together

In a metal structure metal ions are surrounded by a cloud or 'sea' of electrons.

The table below lists materials ranging from the best conductor to the best insulator. The range in the resistance of different materials is truly amazing. Silver is about 10^{27} times better at conducting electricity than the plastic Teflon®. So to replace a 1 mm diameter wire of silver or copper in an electrical circuit, you would need a bar of Teflon far larger in diameter than the Moon's orbit around the Earth.

Silver	metal	conductor (best)
Copper	metal	conductor
Aluminium	metal	conductor
Iron	metal	conductor
Graphite		conductor
Silicon		semiconductor
Most plastics		insulator
Oil		insulator
Glass		insulator
Teflon®		insulator (best)

EFFECTS OF LENGTH AND CROSS-SECTIONAL AREA

For a particular conductor, the resistance is **proportional to length.**
The longer the conductor, the further the electrons have to travel, the
more likely they are to collide with the metal ions and so the greater
the resistance. So a wire that is twice as long will have twice as much
resistance.

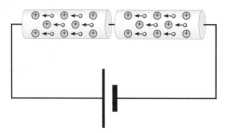

*Two wires in series are like
one long wire, because the
electrons have to travel
twice as far.*

Resistance is **inversely proportional to cross-sectional area.** The greater
the cross-sectional area of the conductor, the more electrons there are
available to carry the charge along the conductor's length and so the
lower the resistance. So a wire with twice the cross-sectional area will
have half the resistance. (Remember that if the wire is of twice the
diameter, then its cross-sectional area will be four times greater, and so
the resistance of the wire will be one quarter as much.)

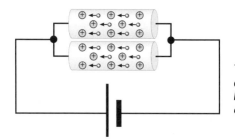

*Two wires in parallel are like
one thick wire, so the electrons
have more routes to travel
along the same distance.*

Charging insulators by friction

Materials like glass, acetate and polythene can only become charged with
static electricity because they are insulators. Electrons do not move easily
through insulating materials, so when extra electrons are added, they stay
on the surface instead of flowing away, and the surface stays negatively
charged. Similarly, if electrons are removed, electrons from other parts of
the material do not flow in to replace them, so the surface stays positively
charged. Conductors, such as metals, cannot be charged with static
electricity by rubbing.

Charge as the loss or gain of electrons

All atoms are made up of three main kinds of particles, called electrons,
protons and neutrons. Electrons are the tiniest of these, and have a
negative charge. Protons and neutrons have about the same mass, but
protons are positively charged, while neutrons have no charge.

In most objects there are as many electrons as protons. So normally an object has no overall charge, because the positive charge on all the protons is matched by the negative charge on the electrons. If there are more electrons than protons the object carries an overall negative charge. If there are fewer electrons than protons, the object carries an overall positive charge.

When you charge an object with static electricity, you are giving or taking away negatively charged electrons, so that the charge on the object overall is unbalanced. For example, when you rub a glass or acetate rod with a cloth, electrons from the rod get rubbed onto the cloth. So the cloth becomes negatively charged overall, and the rod is left with an overall positive charge.

When you rub a polythene rod with a cloth, electrons from the cloth get transferred to the rod, so the polythene carries a negative charge overall, and the cloth carries a positive charge.

A* EXTRA

- The amount of charge on an object is measured in coulombs. A charge of 1C is the charge on 6.2×10^{18} electrons, so an object with a charge of +1.0 C has 6.2×10^{18} too few electrons. This is an enormous charge, and objects would explode long before they could be given so much. Typical electrostatic charges are less than 1 μC $(1.0 \times 10^{-6}C)$.

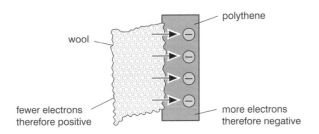

wool — polythene

fewer electrons therefore positive — more electrons therefore negative

Attraction and repulsion

Every proton and electron produces an electric field. So around any object in which the charges are not balanced, there is an electric field. When a charged particle moves into the field, it feels a force towards or away from the other particle (see below). The strength of the force depends on:

- how close the particles are: the closer they are, the larger the force

- how much electrical charge they carry: the more charge, the larger the force.

Like charges repel each other.

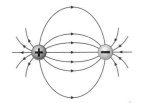

Unlike charges attract each other.

Field lines show the shape of an electric field.

Because the static charge on each hair is similar, the hairs repel each other and stick up in all directions.

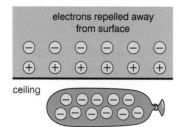

electrons repelled away
from surface

ceiling

negative balloon

The balloon induces a charge
on the ceiling's surface.

When an unbalanced charge collects on the surface of an object, the charge is called static electricity. ('Static' means 'not moving'.) When electrons move, or flow, from one place to another, they produce an electric current.

If you suspended charged polythene and acetate rods so they could move freely, and brought the two close together, they would attract each other, since unlike charges attract.

Similarly, when a balloon is rubbed against clothing it will 'stick' to a wall or ceiling. This is because of the attraction between the negative charges on the balloon and the induced positive charges on the ceiling.

Electrostatics

As you can see, these forces, which are called **electrostatic forces**, look rather similar to magnetic forces. They are however completely different. An electric field does not affect a magnet in any special way, and a magnetic field does not affect an electric charge (so long as it is not moving). You can even have a space that contains both types of field in different directions at the same time.

All the phenomena of electrostatics can be explained in terms of moving negative or moving positive charges. Early scientists did not know which it was, and it was only towards the end of the 19th century that they became sure that it was the negative charges that moved.

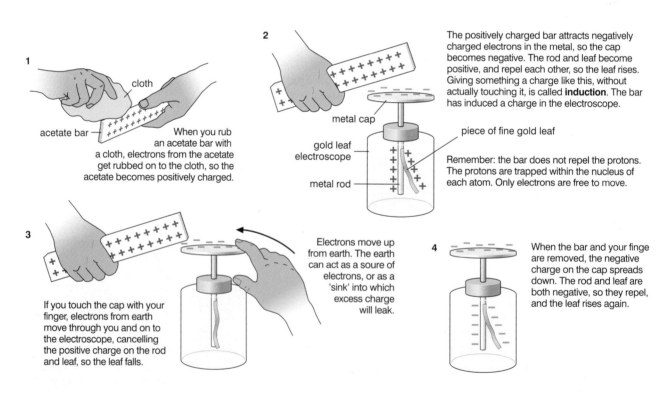

1

cloth

acetate bar

When you rub an acetate bar with a cloth, electrons from the acetate get rubbed on to the cloth, so the acetate becomes positively charged.

2

The positively charged bar attracts negatively charged electrons in the metal, so the cap becomes negative. The rod and leaf become positive, and repel each other, so the leaf rises. Giving something a charge like this, without actually touching it, is called **induction**. The bar has induced a charge in the electroscope.

metal cap

gold leaf electroscope

piece of fine gold leaf

metal rod

Remember: the bar does not repel the protons. The protons are trapped within the nucleus of each atom. Only electrons are free to move.

3

Electrons move up from earth. The earth can act as a soure of electrons, or as a 'sink' into which excess charge will leak.

If you touch the cap with your finger, electrons from earth move through you and on to the electroscope, cancelling the positive charge on the rod and leaf, so the leaf falls.

4

When the bar and your finge are removed, the negative charge on the cap spreads down. The rod and leaf are both negative, so they repel, and the leaf rises again.

Charging an electroscope by induction.

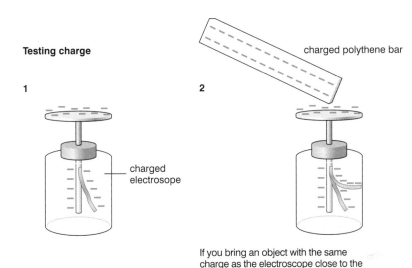

Testing charge

charged polythene bar

charged acetate bar

1

2

3

charged electrosope

Electrons get attracted up to the cap, away from the leaf.

If you bring an object with the same charge as the electroscope close to the cap, the leaf rises further. The more charge on the object, the further the leaf rises.

If you bring an object with the opposite charge to the electroscope close to the cap, the leaf falls. The more charge on the object, the further the leaf falls.

You can use an electroscope to test if an object is positively or negatively charged.

Hazards of electrostatics

The sudden discharge of electricity caused by friction between two insulators can cause shocks in everyday situations – for example:
- combing your hair
- pulling clothes over your head
- getting out of a car.

You may have noticed that you can get a nasty spark from your finger if you touch a metal object after rubbing your feet on a nylon carpet. It is for this reason that people who are manufacturing sensitive electronic devices connect themselves to ground before starting work. And for fear of sparks of this type aircraft are connected to the ground by a special wire before refuelling starts.

Using an antistatic wrist strap.

Lightning is a spectacular example of electrostatics in action. We believe that the electrical charge is generated by induction when ice particles in the clouds collide. One bolt of lightning is about 5 C of electrical charge. Lightning conductors on buildings usually prevent lightning strikes by discharging the cloud above, but if a strike still occurs it is carried safely to ground.

Uses of electrostatics

Electrostatics can be useful: electrostatic scrubbers remove the dust from the smoke of coal power stations, and photocopiers use electrostatics to move the ink powder to the right place on the paper. Electrostatic charges on the filter in an air cleaner or in a vacuum cleaner are responsible for much of the filter's effectiveness.

The electrostatic inkjet printer is used industrially to label the sell-by date onto the cans or bottles passing by on a conveyer belt. In this printer, a nozzle continuously produces a jet of droplets at a very high speed (50 m/s). The droplets are either collected up by the printer – or they are aimed at the cans – by using the fact that each droplet is given a small charge by friction as it passes through the nozzle. The printer can then steer the droplet by applying voltages to metal plates fixed near to the jet. (The inkjet printer for the PC is much simpler, and uses small electrical heaters to squirt ink out of nozzles as the ink head passes over the places where ink is needed on the paper.)

The properties of static electricity are put to good effect in **ink jet printers** and **photocopiers.**

In a photocopier, charged particles attract the toner. Light is used to remove charge from parts that are not to be printed.

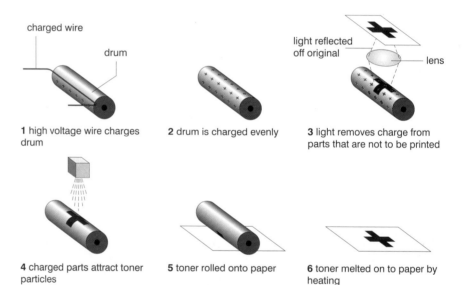

1 high voltage wire charges drum

2 drum is charged evenly

3 light removes charge from parts that are not to be printed

4 charged parts attract toner particles

5 toner rolled onto paper

6 toner melted on to paper by heating

In ink jet printers, uncharged ink droplets do not reach the paper. This is how the spaces between words are made.

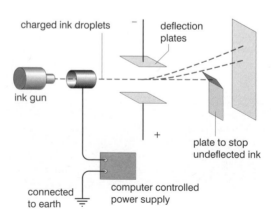

REVIEW QUESTIONS

Q1 A plastic rod is rubbed with a cloth.
  a How does the plastic become positively charged?
  b The charged plastic rod attracts small pieces of paper. Explain why this attraction occurs.

Q2 **a** A car stops and one of the passengers gets out. When she touches a metal post she feels an electric shock. Explain why she feels this shock.
  b Write down two other situations where people might get this type of shock.

Q3 Give two examples of where static electricity can be dangerous.

More questions on the CD ROM

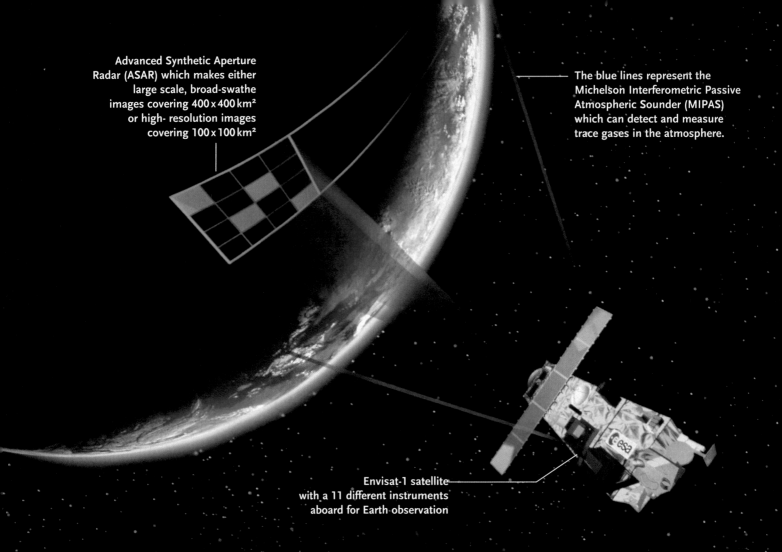

Advanced Synthetic Aperture Radar (ASAR) which makes either large scale, broad-swathe images covering 400 x 400 km² or high-resolution images covering 100 x 100 km²

The blue lines represent the Michelson Interferometric Passive Atmospheric Sounder (MIPAS) which can detect and measure trace gases in the atmosphere.

Envisat-1 satellite with a 11 different instruments aboard for Earth observation

Eyes in the sky

You probably know that artificial satellites orbit the Earth. You can probably describe some ways in which the satellites are used. But you might be surprised at just how many uses there are. Did you realise that some newspapers send their text and pictures to different printing sites via satellite? This saves on distribution time and costs and allows the newspaper to keep up as up to date with news stories as possible. You are probably aware of the Global Positioning System (GPS) that allows ships and planes to know their exact position on the Earth's surface, but did you realise the same system is used to track packages being delivered by trucks and is even used to tell when the drivers are driving too fast?

Satellite images use many different wavelengths of radiation, for example, visible wavelengths and infrared. They show different features of the surface beneath them, for example, some wavelengths are reflected by clouds and are useful in weather forecasting. Next time you see a weather forecast showing satellites images taken during the night, see if you can work out how the picture was taken. Wasn't it dark at the time?

There are many, many other applications of satellite imaging, from spying to search and rescue, from surveying to earthquake monitoring. Satellites come in different sizes and orbit the Earth in different paths. Why not spend a little time researching this interesting and constantly changing topic?

WAVES

Satellite image of Singapore and surroundings
taken by NASA's *Landsat 7*
combining infrared and visible light

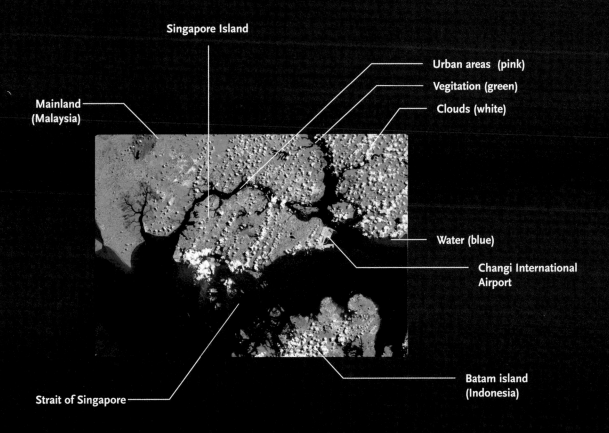

Singapore Island

Mainland
(Malaysia)

Urban areas (pink)

Vegitation (green)

Clouds (white)

Water (blue)

Changi International
Airport

Batam island
(Indonesia)

Strait of Singapore

PROPERTIES OF WAVES

The behaviour of waves affects us every second of our lives. Waves are reaching us constantly: sound waves, light waves, infrared heat, television, mobile-phone and radio waves, the list goes on. The study of waves is, perhaps, truly the central subject of physics.

Longitudinal and transverse waves

There are two types of waves: longitudinal and transverse.

Longitudinal waves. This type of wave can be shown by pushing and pulling a spring. The spring stretches in places and squashes in others. The stretching produces regions of **rarefaction**, whilst the squashing produces regions of **compression**. Sound is an example of a longitudinal wave.

Transverse waves. In a transverse wave the vibrations are at right angles to the direction of motion. Light, radio and other electromagnetic waves are transverse waves.

In the examples below, the waves are very narrow, and are confined to the spring or the string that they are travelling down. Most waves are not confined in this way. Clearly a single wave on the sea, for example, can be hundreds of metres wide as it moves along.

Water waves are often used to demonstrate the properties of waves because the **wavefront** of a water wave is easy to see. A wavefront is the moving line that joins all the points on the crest of a wave.

This student can feel the heat waves from the Sun coming in through the windows of the train, she can hear the sound waves of her friend on the phone, the phone is using radio waves, and she can see around her with light waves.

Longitudinal and transverse waves are made by vibrations. Both types of wave have a repeating shape or pattern.

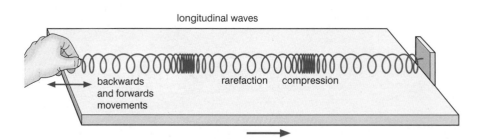

longitudinal waves

backwards and forwards movements

rarefaction   compression

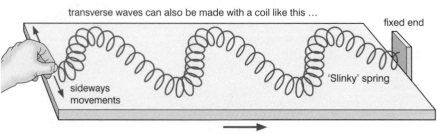

transverse waves can also be made with a coil like this ...

fixed end

sideways movements

'Slinky' spring

direction of wave travel

Amplitude, frequency, wavelength and period.

Waves have a wavelength, frequency, amplitude and time period.

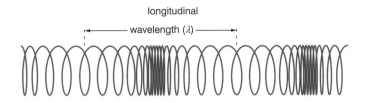

The **wavelength** is the distance between two peaks or, if you prefer, the distance between two troughs of the wave. In the case of longitudinal waves, it is the distance between two points of maximum compression, or the distance between two points of minimum compression.

The **frequency** is the number of peaks (or the number of troughs) that go past each second.

The **time period** is the time taken for each complete cycle of the wave motion.

The **amplitude** is the maximum displacement of the medium's vibration. In transverse waves, this is half the crest-to-trough height.

The **speed** of the wave is simply the speed of the wave as it approaches. The speed depends on the substance or medium the wave is passing through.

The largest ocean wave measured accurately had a wavelength of 340 m, a frequency of 0.067 Hz (that is to say one peak every 15 s), and a speed of 23 m/s. The amplitude of the wave was 17 m, so the ship that was measuring the wave was going 17 m above the level of a smooth sea and then 17 m below. (The waves were 34 m from crest to trough.)

Waves transfer energy and information

A wave carries energy, and can carry information. You can feel the energy in infrared waves from the Sun as they strike your hands; you can see the energy contained in the ocean waves from a typhoon as they reach the coast after travelling hundreds of miles. And you can see the information contained in the light reaching your eyes from this page, or from a movie screen.

But note that in none of these cases has any object or matter travelled from the source of the waves to the destination. Instead the wave is passed on from point to point along the route taken by the wave. One good example is a piece of wood in the sea. It is jiggled up and down, and to and fro, by a wave, but after the wave has passed it ends up where it started.

(A surfer can travel by catching a wave and 'riding it', but he is outside the wave and not part of it!)

Relationship between speed, frequency and wavelength

The speed of a wave in a given medium is constant. If you change the wavelength, the frequency *must* change as well. If you imagine that some waves are going past you on a spring or on a rope, then they will be going at a constant speed. If the waves get closer together, then more waves must go past you each second, and that means that the frequency has gone up. The speed, frequency and wavelength of a wave are related by the equation:

wave speed = frequency × wavelength

$v = f \times \lambda$

   v = wave speed, usually measured in metres/second (m/s)

   f = frequency, measured in cycles per second or hertz (Hz)

   λ = wavelength, usually measured in metres (m)

Relationship between frequency and time period

The **time period** (T) is the time taken for each complete cycle of the wave motion. It is closely linked to the frequency (f) by this relationship:

$$\text{frequency (in hertz, Hz)} = \frac{1}{\text{time period (in seconds, s)}} \quad \text{or } f = \frac{1}{T}$$

Using the relationships

WORKED EXAMPLES

1 A loudspeaker makes sound waves with a frequency of 300 Hz. The waves have a wavelength of 1.13 m. Calculate the speed of the waves.

Write down the formula:	$v = f \times \lambda$
Substitute the values for f and λ:	$v = 300 \times 1.13$
Work out the answer and write down the unit:	$v = 339$ m/s

2 A radio station broadcasts on a wavelength of 250 m. The speed of the radio waves is 3×10^8 m/s. Calculate the frequency.

Write down the formula with f as the subject:	$f = \dfrac{v}{\lambda}$
Substitute the values for v and λ:	$f = \dfrac{3 \times 10^8}{250}$
Work out the answer and write down the unit:	$f = 1\,200\,000$ Hz or 1200 kHz

3 A tuning fork is used to play a middle C, which has a frequency of 256 Hz. Calculate the time period of the vibration.

Write down the formula with T as the subject:	$T = \dfrac{1}{f}$
Substitute the value of f:	$T = \dfrac{1}{256}$
Work out the answer and write down the unit:	$T = 0.0039$ s

Reflection, refraction and diffraction

When a wave hits a barrier the wave will be **reflected**. If it hits the barrier at an angle then the **angle of reflection** will be **equal** to the **angle of incidence**. **Echoes** are a common consequence of the reflection of sound waves.

When a wave moves from one medium into another, it will either speed up or slow down. For example, a wave going along a rope will speed up if the rope becomes thinner. (This is why you can 'crack' a whip.) And sound going from cold air to hotter air will speed up. When a wave **slows down**, the wavefronts crowd together – the **wavelength gets smaller**. When a wave **speeds up**, the wavefronts spread out – the **wavelength gets larger**. Note that in both cases, the same number of waves will pass you per second; the wavelength may have changed, but the frequency has not.

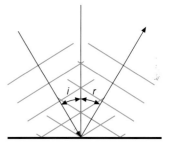

Waves hit a barrier at an angle of incidence *i*. The waves bounce off with the angle of incidence *i* equal to the angle of reflection *r*. The reflected wave is the same shape as the incident wave.

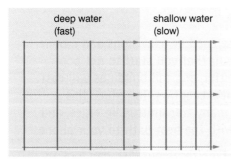

When waves slow down, their wavelength gets shorter.

This surfer is successfully travelling along one wavefront. The next wavefront looks very close behind, but is probably still 50 m away. (This is an illusion caused by telephoto camera lenses.)

If a wave enters a new medium at an angle then the wavefronts also change direction. This is known as **refraction**. The amount that the wave is bent by depends on the change in speed. Water waves are slower in shallower water than in deep water, so water waves will refract when the depth changes.

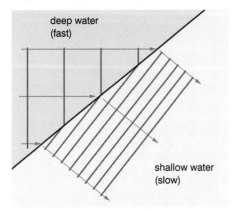

If waves cross into a new medium at an angle, their wavelength and direction change.

A* EXTRA

- High notes from a CD track have wavelengths of around 10–20 cm. For these to diffract efficiently and spread out as they leave the opening of the loudspeaker, a speaker with a smaller diameter is used. For lower notes, which have larger wavelengths, a speaker with a larger diameter is used in order to generate enough volume.

Wavefronts change shape when they pass the edge of an obstacle or go through a gap. This process is known as **diffraction**. Diffraction is strong when the width of the gap is similar in size to the wavelength of the waves.

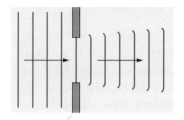 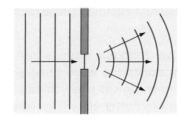

Diffraction is most noticeable when the size of the gap equals the wavelength of the waves.

Diffraction is a problem in communications when radio and television signals are transmitted through the air in a narrow beam. Diffraction of the wavefront means that not all the energy transmitted with the wavefront reaches the receiving dishes.

Short-wavelength signals, such as those used in televisions and mobile phones, diffract very little, with the result that you start to get poor reception if you cannot see the transmitter, and tall buildings will cast shadows that will make it difficult to get reception. To reduce this problem, mobile phone companies use many transmitters in cities, and switch your phone to the transmitter with the best path to your phone.

Satellite television has the great advantage that your dish can look up in the sky at the satellite and get a direct view of it.

On the other hand, diffraction allows long-wave radio waves to spread out and diffract around buildings and hills.

REVIEW QUESTIONS

Q1 A sound wave is observed on a cathode ray oscilloscope. It has a simple smooth repeating pattern.
Draw a suitable trace of a sound wave and label it to indicate:
- **a** the crest of the wave
- **b** the wavelength of the wave
- **c** the amplitude of the wave.

The frequency of the wave is 512 Hz. How many waves are produced each second?

Q2 Radio waves of frequency 900 MHz are used to send information to and from a portable phone. The speed of the waves is 3×10^8 m/s. Calculate the wavelength of the waves.
(1 MHz = 1 000 000 Hz, 3×10^8 = 300 000 000.)

Q3 What are the most likely explanations of the following effects? Explain carefully.

a The captain of an ocean-going ship is proceeding slowly into waves that are coming towards the ship. He suddenly notices that the waves change in two ways about 200 m ahead of where the ship is. They get further apart and change direction quite noticeably.

b An observer is standing on the bank of a river. The wind is blowing from left to right, and waves are moving from left to right. However, the observer sees a small piece of wood that is moving slowly from right to left as it floats in the middle of the river .

c You find that you can listen to radio stations in all of the rooms in your home, but you cannot get a mobile phone signal in certain rooms even if you open the windows.

More questions on the CD ROM

THE ELECTROMAGNETIC SPECTRUM

Videos & questions on the CD ROM

The **electromagnetic spectrum** is a 'family' of waves. Electromagnetic waves all travel at the same speed in a vacuum, i.e. the speed of light, 300 000 000 m/s. This can be written more conveniently as 3×10^8 m/s. This high speed explains why you can have a phone call between China and New Zealand with only an extra delay of 0.1 s before you hear the reply from the person at the other end. It takes the infrared signal this long to travel there and back through an optical fibre.

However, for astronomical distances the delays quickly become longer. Even when Mars is at its nearest to Earth, it takes 10 minutes to send a message to a robot on the surface and receive a reply. Getting a reply from the nearest star would take $8\frac{1}{2}$ years.

Note that all electromagnetic waves can travel through a vacuum, which is why we can see the light and feel the heat coming from the Sun. Other waves, such as sound waves, cannot travel through a vacuum.

Order of the electromagnetic spectrum

A prism splits white light into the colourful spectrum of visible light.

White light is a mixture of different colours and can be split by a prism into the **visible spectrum**. All the different colours of light travel at the same speed in a vacuum but they have different frequencies and wavelengths. Red light has a wavelength that is about twice as long as violet light. When the colours enter glass or perspex they all slow down, but by different amounts. The different colours are therefore refracted through different angles. Violet is refracted the most, red the least.

The visible spectrum is only a small part of the full electromagnetic spectrum.

The visible light region of the spectrum contains the colours ranged from red, through orange, yellow, green and blue to violet. The red lies next to infrared, and violet is next to the ultraviolet.

Light of one wavelength, that is to say of just one colour, is known as **monochromatic** light.

The complete electromagnetic spectrum.

Type of wave	gamma rays	X-rays	ultraviolet	visible	infrared	microwaves	TV and radio waves
Frequency	high						low
Wavelength	low						high
Use	killing cancer cells	to look at bones	sun tan beds	photography	TV remote controls	cooking	transmission of TV and radio

Uses and hazards of electromagnetic radiation

This section looks at the uses of different types of electromagnetic radiation. It also discusses the harmful effects on the human body caused by excessive exposure to electromagnetic waves.

Gamma rays are produced by radioactive nuclei. They transfer more energy than X-rays and can cause cancer or mutation in body cells. Gamma rays are frequently used in radiotherapy to kill cancer cells. The success of this treatment is greatly improved by the fact that cancer cells are easier to kill than ordinary cells.

Radioactive substances that emit gamma rays are used as tracers. For example, if scientists want to know where in a plant the phosphorus goes, they can feed it a radioactive isotope of phosphorus and then measure the radioactivity that comes out of different parts of the plant.

X-rays are produced when high-energy electrons are fired at a metal target. Bones absorb more X-rays than other body tissue. If a person is placed between the X-ray source and a photographic plate, the bones appear to be white on the developed photographic plate compared with the rest of the body. X-rays have very high energy and can damage or destroy body cells. They may also cause cancer. X-rays are also used to treat cancer.

Ultraviolet radiation (UV) is the component of the Sun's rays that gives you a suntan. UV is also created in fluorescent light tubes by exciting the atoms in a mercury vapour. The UV radiation is then absorbed by the coating on the inside of the fluorescent tube and re-emitted as visible light. Fluorescent tubes are more efficient than light bulbs because they do not depend on heating and so more energy is available to produce light. Ultraviolet can also damage the surface cells of the body, which can lead to skin cancer, and can damage the eyes, leading to blindness.

All objects give out **infrared radiation** (IR). The hotter the object is, the more radiation it gives out. Thermograms are photographs taken to show the infrared radiation given out from objects. Infrared radiation grills and cooks our food in an ordinary oven and is used in remote controls to operate televisions and videos. Infrared can burn skin and other body tissue.

Microwaves are high-frequency radio waves. They are used in radar to find the position of airplanes and ships. Metal objects reflect the microwaves back to the transmitter, enabling the distance between the object and the transmitter to be calculated. Microwaves are also used for cooking. Water particles in food absorb the energy carried by microwaves. They vibrate more and get much hotter. Microwaves penetrate several centimetres into the food and so speed up the cooking process. Because of this, microwaves can heat body tissue internally.

Radio waves have the longest wavelengths and lowest frequencies. **UHF** (ultra-high frequency) waves are used to transmit television programmes to homes. **VHF** (very high frequency) waves are used to transmit local radio programmes. **Medium** and **long** radio waves are used to transmit over longer distances because their wavelengths allow them to diffract around obstacles such as buildings and hills. Communication satellites above the Earth receive signals carried by high-frequency (**short-wave**) radio waves. These signals are amplified and re-transmitted to other parts of the world.

A* EXTRA

- The energy associated with an electromagnetic wave depends on its frequency. The waves with the higher frequencies are potentially the more hazardous.

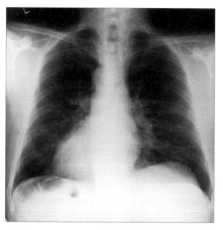

An X-ray may save your life, but it is not free from danger. A doctor will only arrange for an X-ray when it is clear that the benefits to you are far greater than the tiny risk that it will make you ill.

A* EXTRA

- Infrared radiation is absorbed by the surface of the food and the energy is spread through the rest of the food by conduction.
- In contrast, microwaves penetrate a few centimetres into food and then the energy is transferred throughout the food by conduction.

QUESTIONS

Q1 This is a list of types of wave:
gamma infrared microwaves radio ultraviolet visible X-rays
Choose from the list the type of wave that best fits each of these descriptions.
a Stimulates the sensitive cells at the back of the eye.
b Necessary for a suntan.
c Used for rapid cooking in an oven.
d Used to take a photograph of the bones in a broken arm.
e Emitted by a video remote control unit.

Q2 Gamma rays are part of the electromagnetic spectrum. Gamma rays are useful to us but can also be very dangerous.
a Explain how the properties of gamma rays make them useful to us.
b Explain why gamma rays can cause damage to people.
c Give one difference between microwaves and gamma rays.
d Microwaves travel at 300 000 000 m/s. What speed do gamma rays travel at?

More questions on the CD ROM

Q3 a Write down the parts of the electromagnetic spectrum in order of increasing wavelength.
b How would your list be different if you wrote it in order of increasing frequency?

LIGHT AND SOUND

Videos & questions
on the CD ROM

Light waves

Light waves have all of the properties of waves. We have already discussed their speed and their wavelength. In addition, they are transverse waves. So, as a light wave approaches your eye, it may be **vertically polarised** and oscillating up and down (a bit like an ocean wave) or it may be **horizontally polarised** and oscillating from side to side. Light from an ordinary lamp contains both of these types, but reflections from the surface of water or glass may be just one type, a fact that is obvious to wearers of polarising sunglasses. (Polarising sunglasses only accept light waves that are vertically polarised, and sunlight reflected from the sea or river is horizontally polarised.)

Like all other waves, light can be reflected, refracted and diffracted. Reflection and refraction are easy to demonstrate with a mirror and a glass of water. The effects of diffraction are very hard to see. The effects are small because the wavelength of light is so short.

Reflection of light and ray diagrams

A ray of light is a line drawn to show the path that the light waves take.

We need to study what happens when an incident light ray (a light ray that is going to fall on a surface) hits a mirror and is reflected off.

Light rays are reflected from mirrors in such a way that

angle of incidence (*i*) = angle of reflection (*r*)

The angles are measured to an imaginary line at 90° to the surface of the mirror. This line is called the **normal**. With a curved mirror it is difficult to measure the angle between the ray and the mirror, but the same law still applies.

When you look in a plane mirror you see an **image** of yourself. The image is said to be **laterally inverted** because if you raise your right hand your image raises what you would call its left hand. The image is formed as far behind the mirror as you are in front of it and is the same size as you. The image cannot be projected onto a screen. It is known as a **virtual image**.

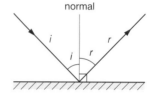

The angles of incidence and reflection are the same when a mirror reflects light. The type of curved mirror below is known as a convex mirror.

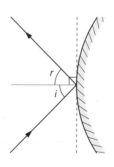

As you look at the face of the boy and his image in the mirror, you can see that every part of his face is directly opposite its image in the mirror, and that each part is the same distance away from the mirror as its image.

Rays of light travel outwards from the lamp in all directions. Here just two rays are drawn to show how light goes from the lamp to the observer's eye. After the rays have reflected from the mirror, they travel along lines that look *as if* they started from the image. The eye is tricked into thinking that the light really did start from the image.

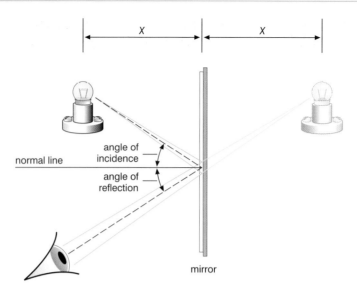

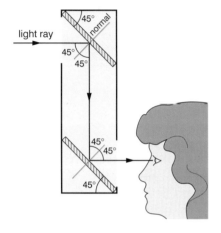

A periscope uses reflection to allow you to see above your normal line of vision – or even round corners.

In a plane mirror the image is always the same size as the object. Examples of plane mirrors include household 'dressing' mirrors, dental mirrors for examining teeth, security mirrors for checking under vehicles, periscope.

Close to a **concave mirror** the image is **larger** than the object – these mirrors **magnify**. They are used in make-up and shaving mirrors. They are used in torches and car headlamps to produce a beam of light.

The image in a **convex mirror** is always **smaller** than the object. Examples are a car driving mirror and a shop security mirror.

Refraction of light

Light waves **slow down** when they travel from air into glass. If they are at an angle to the glass, they bend towards the normal. When the light rays travel out of the glass into the air, their speed increases and they bend away from the normal. If the block of glass has parallel sides, the light resumes its original direction. This is why a sheet of window glass has so little effect on the view beyond. However, the view is shifted slightly sideways if you are looking through the glass at an angle.

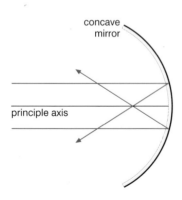

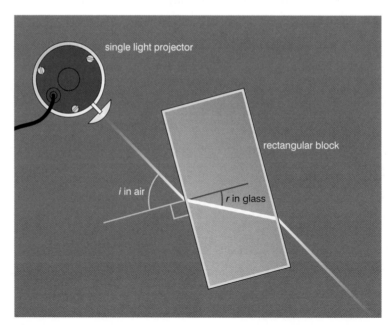

The angle of incidence i, is the angle between the incident light ray and the normal to the surface. The angle of refraction r is the angle between the refracted light ray and the normal to the surface inside the material.

(Note that people tend to use the letter r both for the angle of reflection and the angle of refraction. But it will be clear from the context whether they are talking about reflection or refraction.)

Refractive index

The **refractive index** of a material indicates how strongly the material changes the direction of the light. It is calculated using the following formula:

$$\text{refractive index } n = \frac{\sin i}{\sin r}$$

i = angle of incidence

r = angle of refraction

The refractive index of a vacuum is 1, and the refractive index of air is fractionally higher, but we will take it as 1. Other common refractive indices are water 1.3; window glass 1.5; sapphire 1.75; diamond 2.4. The high refractive index of diamond explains why it 'sparkles' so much.

The refractive index n can also be defined as:

$$n = \frac{\text{speed of light in vacuum (or air)}}{\text{speed of light in the material}}$$

Measuring the refractive index of a glass block

1   Place a piece of paper on a wooden surface, and put a glass block on the paper.

2   Draw on the paper round the perimeter of the glass block. (Be careful not to move the block after this.)

3   Set up a light box as shown opposite. Push two pins through the paper and into the wooden surface along the light beam between lamp and glass block.

4   Push two pins into the path of the light beam after the glass block.

5   Remove the glass block and the pins. You can now draw a line all the way along the path of the light, including the path through the block.

6   At the point where the light enters the glass block, draw a line at 90° to the front of the block.

7   With a protractor, measure the angle of incidence i and the angle of refraction r.

For accuracy, in both cases put one pin close to the block, and one pin as far away from the block as you can reasonably manage.

An alternative method is not to use a light box at all. Instead, put two pins into the paper at step 3, choosing suitable places for yourself. In step 4, lower your head until you can see these pins by looking through the glass block. You then add the second two pins so that all four pins appear to be in a straight line.

WORKED EXAMPLES

1 If the speed of light in a vacuum is 300 000 000 m/s, what is the speed of light in glass with a refractive index of 1.5?

Write down the formula: $n = \dfrac{\text{speed of light in vacuum (or air)}}{\text{speed of light in the material}}$

Rearrange the formula: $\text{speed in material} = \dfrac{\text{speed in vacuum}}{n}$

Substitute the values: $\text{speed in material} = \dfrac{300\ 000\ 000}{1.5}$

Work out the answer and write down the unit:

$$\text{speed of light in the material} = 200\ 000\ 000 \text{ m/s}$$
$$= 2 \times 10^8 \text{ m/s}$$

2 A light ray approaches a block of plastic with an angle of incidence of 60°. If the refractive index of the plastic is 1.4, what is the angle of refraction?

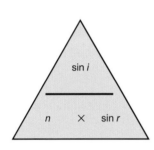

Write down the formula: $n = \dfrac{\sin i}{\sin r}$

If $i = 60°$, $\sin i = 0.866$

Rearrange the formula: $\sin r = \dfrac{\sin i}{n}$

Substitute the values: $\sin r = \dfrac{0.866}{1.4}$

Work out the answer: $\sin r = 0.619$

From a calculator, if $\sin r = 0.619$, then $r = 38.2°$

The angle of refraction is 38.2°.

Total internal reflection and the critical angle

When rays of light pass from a **slow medium** to a **faster medium** they move **away** from the normal.

As the angle of incidence increases, an angle is reached at which the light rays will have to leave with an angle of refraction greater than 90°! These rays cannot refract, so they are entirely reflected back inside the medium. This process is known as **total internal reflection**.

Total internal reflection occurs when a ray of light tries to leave the glass. If the angle of incidence equals or is greater than the critical angle the ray will be totally internally reflected. In this picture, the angle is 2 or 3º less than the critical angle, and light is just managing to escape from the glass.

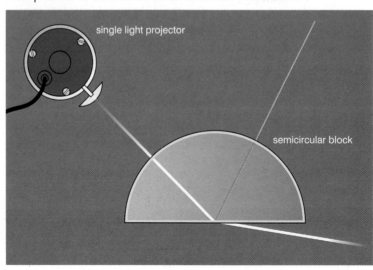

single light projector

semicircular block

The angle of incidence at which all refraction stops is known as the **critical angle** for the material.

The critical angle, c, is linked to the refractive index by this formula:

$$\sin c = \frac{1}{n}$$

So, for window glass, refractive index 1.5, we find that c = =1/1.5 = 0.67. The critical angle for the window glass is therefore approximately 42°. Similarly, the critical angle for water is 49°.

Total internal reflection is used in **fibre-optic cables**. A fibre-optic cable is made of a single glass fibre. The light continues along the fibre by being constantly internally reflected.

Light does not escape from the fibre because it always hits it at an angle greater than the critical angle and is internally reflected.

Telephone and TV communications systems are increasingly relying on fibre optics instead of the more traditional copper cables. Fibre-optic cables do not use electricity – the signals are carried by infrared rays. The signals are very clear as they do not suffer from electrical interference. Other advantages are that they are cheaper than the copper cables and can carry thousands of different signals down the same fibre at the same time.

Bundles of several thousand optical fibres are used in medical endoscopes for internal examination of the body. The bundle will carry an image from one end of the bundle to the other, each fibre carrying one tiny part (one pixel) of the image.

Glass prisms with internal angles of 45°, 45° and 90° are used as mirrors in periscopes and binoculars. In periscopes, light enters the prism through one of the smaller faces, is totally reflected off the inside of the larger face, and leaves through the other smaller face with its direction changed by 90°. Just the plain glass of the prism is used: no metal layer is needed.

Binoculars consist of a pair of telescopes made shorter by 'folding up' the light path between the front and back lenses. Two 45°, 45°, 90° prisms are used, each changing the direction of the light by 180°. Light enters through one side of the larger face of the prism and is reflected off each of the two smaller faces in turn, being bent by 90° each time. It finally emerges from the other side of the prism's larger face, travelling in the opposite direction.

Analogue and digital signals

We receive information from the world around us by means of signals: light, sound, heat, taste etc. These signals vary in a very complex way with time. In the case of sound, for example, the sound waves arriving at our ears cause the air pressure to go up and down in a way that looks almost meaningless, but that the brain has an amazing ability to interpret as speech.

In analogue coding, the processed signal can vary over a range of values. The pattern produced follows the original information.

In digital coding, the processed signal can only take only two values, 1 and 0.

The pressure signal arriving at the ear can have any value at all between the minimum and maximum pressures that are set by the volume control on your personal stereo. A signal that can have any value over a range is known as an **analogue signal**.

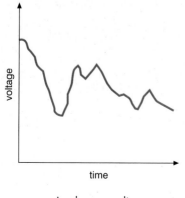

Analogue coding

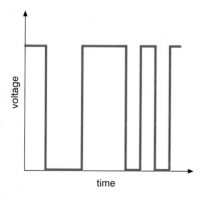

Digital coding

Since the 1980s, signals have tended to become digital rather than analogue. A **digital signal** consists of nothing but a long series of numbers, each one being a 1 or a 0. Each number is known as a **bit**. A computer can turn an analogue signal into a digital one, or back. As you will know, CDs and DVDs store the sound and vision in digital form. It takes a large number of bits to convey a modest amount of information. A DVD player has to read about 5 million bits per second to display the movie picture on the screen.

Why bother with digital signals? Well, they are ideal for sending down optical fibres because it does not matter if the signal is weakened during its journey down the fibre, perhaps a distance of hundreds of kilometres. The detector at the receiving end only has to decide if the signal is 'on' or 'off'.

They are also cheap to store, as is shown by the DVD itself. If you have seen old analogue VHS video recorders you will know how complex they were.

But of course digital signals must always be converted back to analogue before humans can understand the information that they contain.

Sound waves

Sound is caused by vibrations, of the front of a violin or a cello, or of the column of air inside a trumpet. In the case of a loudspeaker it is particularly clear that the cone of the loudspeaker moves in and out and changes the pressure in the air in front of it. The sound travels as **longitudinal waves**. The compressions and rarefactions of sound waves result in small differences in air pressure.

Like other longitudinal waves, sound waves can be reflected, refracted or diffracted.

This orchestra is creating a single longitudinal wave of very complicated shape. In ways that we barely understand, our brains can pick out the sounds of all the individual instruments that are playing together.

Sounds humans can hear

The human ear can detect sounds with pitches ranging from 20 Hz to 20 000 Hz. Sound with frequencies above this range is known as **ultrasound**. Ultrasound is used by bats for navigation and by doctors for looking at unborn babies.

The ear is far more easily damaged than most people realise, and care needs to be taken both with the volume of sound and the length of time that the ear is exposed to it. The damage is cumulative, and so is not noticed at first. Many older rock stars have serious hearing problems, and younger ones often wear ear plugs.

Measuring the speed of sound

Sound waves travel faster through liquids than through air. Sound travels fastest through solids. This is because particles are linked most strongly in solids. Note, however, that sound must have a medium through which to travel. Unlike electromagnetic waves, sound will not travel through a vacuum.

Sound travels much more slowly than light in the air. We can use this to measure how quickly sound travels in air.

A* EXTRA

- The speed of sound in water is about 1500 m/s, and in hard metals and wood it is about 5000 m/s.

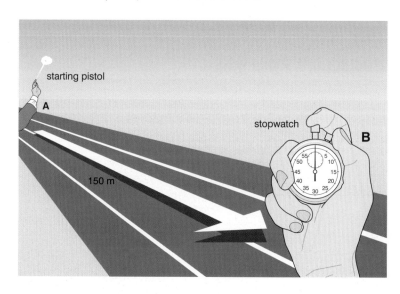

starting pistol

A

stopwatch

B

150 m

Person A makes a loud sound and produces a visual signal at the same time – this could be by firing a starting pistol or by banging large cymbals together. Person B starts a stopwatch when they *see* the sound being made and stops the stopwatch when they *hear* the sound. They can work out the speed of sound using this formula:

$$\text{speed of sound} = \frac{\text{distance between the two people (in m)}}{\text{time measured (in s)}}$$

Sound waves travel at about 340 m/s in the air – much slower than the speed of light. This explains why you almost always see the flash of lightning before hearing the crash of the thunder.

Using an oscilloscope and microphone

Sound waves can be displayed on an oscilloscope by using a microphone. This produces a displacement–time graph for the sound wave.

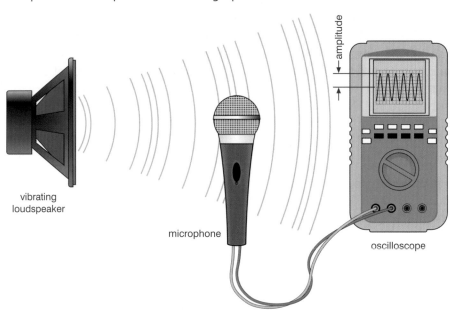

vibrating
loudspeaker

microphone

oscilloscope

FINDING THE FREQUENCY OF A SOUND WAVE

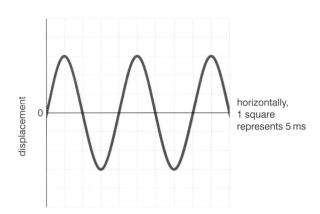

horizontally,
1 square
represents 5 ms

To find out the frequency of a sound wave on an oscilloscope:

1 Adjust the oscilloscope to get a clear stationary trace on the screen.

2 Check the controls of the oscilloscope to see what time is represented by each horizontal square on the screen. In this example, each square represents 5 ms.

3 Check from the screen how often the signal repeats itself. In this case, the time taken for one cycle is 4 squares, or 20 ms. Convert this to seconds: 1 ms = 0.001 s, and so 20 ms = 0.020 s. This is the period of the wave.

4 The frequency is the number of waves per second = 1/period = 1/0.020 = 50 Hz.

Pitch, frequency, amplitude and loudness

High-pitch sounds have a high frequency. Examples of high-pitch sounds include bird-song, and all the sounds that you hear from someone else's personal stereo when they have set the volume too high. Low-pitch sounds have a low frequency. Examples of low-pitch sounds include the horn of a large ship and the bass guitar.

Loud sounds have high amplitude whereas quiet sounds have low amplitude. The loudness of sounds can be compared using decibels.

Typical sound wave patterns are shown on the graphs below.

(a) A loud sound of low frequency

(b) A loud sound of high frequency

(c) A quiet sound of low frequency

(d) A quiet sound of high frequency.

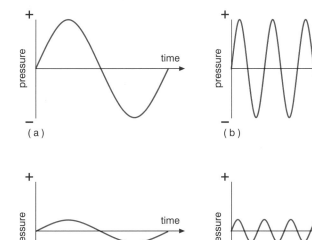

REVIEW QUESTIONS

Q1 a Rays of light can be reflected and refracted. State one difference between reflection and refraction.

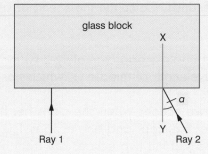

b The diagram shows a glass block and two rays of light.
  i Complete the paths of the two rays as they pass into and then out of the glass block.
  ii What name is given to the angle marked *a*?
  iii What name is given to the line marked XY?

Q2 The diagram shows light entering a prism. Total internal reflection takes place at the inner surfaces of the prism.

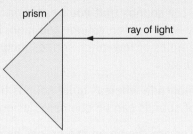

a Complete the path of the ray.
b Suggest one use for a prism like this.
c Complete the table about total internal reflection. Use T for total internal reflection or R for refraction.

Angle of incidence (degrees) at the second face	Total internal reflection (T) or refraction (R)
36	
42 (critical angle)	
46	

Q3 A student traces the path of a red light beam through a rectangular block of plastic, and finds that the angle of incidence is 50°, and the angle of refraction is 21.7°.
a What is the refractive index of the block?
b What will be the critical angle for this material?

Q4 a i What causes a sound?
   ii Explain how sound travels through the air.
b Astronauts in space cannot talk directly to each other. They have to speak to each other by radio. Explain why this is so.
c If a marching band is approaching you, explain why you can hear the bass drum long before you can hear the piccolo playing the highest notes.

Q5 Ayesha and Salma are doing an experiment to measure the speed of sound. They stand 150 m apart.
Ayesha starts the stopwatch when she sees Salma make a sound and she stops it when she hears the sound herself. She measures the time as 0.44 seconds. Calculate the speed of sound in air from this data.

Q6 The speed of sound in air is approximately 340 m/s.
a Calculate the wavelength of middle C, which has a frequency of 256 Hz.
b A student hears two echoes when she claps her hands. One echo is 0.5 s after the clap, and one echo is 1.0 s after the clap. She decides that the two echoes are from two buildings directly in front of her. How far apart are the buildings?

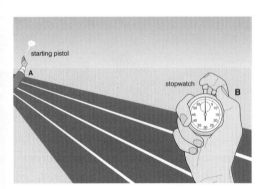

starting pistol
A
stopwatch
B

More questions on the CD ROM

Energy for today and tomorrow

Predicting the future can be a tricky thing. One thing that is certain is that we will continue to need considerable energy supplies. The use of fossil fuels is coming under increasing pressure, both in terms of long-term supply and carbon emissions. Nuclear power continues to present difficulties, both technological and political. With this background, increasing the use of renewable energy sources makes environmental and economic sense. In 2005, South-East Asia's first wind farm was opened in the Philippines, in Ilocos Norte about 500 km north of Manilla.

Rated at 25 MW, the wind farm is a first step along a road that many hope will see further development. Also in 2005, South Korea opened its first wind farm and China passed a Renewable Energy Law, declaring its target of providing 20 000 MW of wind power by 2020.

However, some people have concerns about such an expansion of wind power. Suitable sites are often away from where the energy is needed, so roads have to be built and new power lines constructed. Maintenance can be difficult and expensive. To produce the equivalent of a traditional power station, wind farms need to be very large in. Concerns have also been expressed about the effect of wind farms on birds and even aquatic mammals as the motion of the blades can send vibrations through the water.

The physics of energy resources and energy transfer helps us to better understand the possibilities so that the decisions we make are informed ones.

ENERGY RESOURCES AND ENERGY TRANSFER

ENERGY TRANSFER

Videos & questions on the CD ROM

Fuel, whatever form it comes in, gives a car the ability to move.

These electric streetcars take electrical energy from the overhead wire and convert it into kinetic energy.

Energy

If you own a car, it will not move without fuel. At present this fuel could be petrol or alcohol or diesel fuel. In the past the fuel could, just possibly, have been coal; and in the future it could be hydrogen, or electricity stored in a battery. But whatever fuel you use, you are buying something with the ability to make that car move. This stored ability is known as potential energy.

A clock needs energy to make the hands move, and this energy can be stored in a spring that you wind up with a key, in an electrical battery, or in weights that are raised up.

Stored, or hidden, energy is called **potential energy**. In this context 'potential' does not mean 'with qualities that may lead to future success' (as in 'potential film star') but rather 'containing power'. If a spring is stretched, the spring will have potential energy. If a load is raised above the ground, it will have **gravitational potential energy**.

If the spring is released or the load moves back to the ground, the stored potential energy is transferred to movement energy, which is called **kinetic energy**.

In all of the examples above, the potential energy can be used to make an object move, and hence give it kinetic energy. Kinetic energy can also be transferred into potential energy, and this can be seen most clearly in the action of a pendulum, where at each end of its swing the pendulum has a maximum amount of gravitational potential energy, and at the middle of its swing where some of the potential energy has been used (the pendulum is lower down) and transferred into kinetic energy (the pendulum is moving fastest).

DIFFERENT FORMS OF ENERGY

As can be seen in the pendulum, energy can either be stored or can be seen in motion in some way.

The different types of stored energy are all forms of **potential energy**. Here are some important examples:

Potential energy due to gravity

This is energy stored by an object being raised up in a gravitational field, for example a ball on top of a hill.

'Strain energy'

The word 'strain' means stretched. 'Strain energy' can be stored in springs (in clocks, for example) and in bows when they are drawn back before the arrow is released.

'Chemical energy'

The energy stored in fuels such as petrol and diesel is usually called 'chemical energy'. In any object the atoms are held together by forces that are called bonds. These bonds behave like springs. In some materials, such as fuels and explosives, the bonds are forced to be shorter or longer than they wish. This stores energy in the bonds that can be released by breaking up the structure of the fuel or the explosive.

A battery is ready to turn 'chemical energy' into 'electrical energy', and a rechargeable battery is so called because every time that it is discharged it can be recharged by forcing electricity through it backwards. The 'electrical energy' that is fed is stored as 'chemical energy'.

'Nuclear energy'

The energy in a nucleus of an atom is stored in the extremely strong bonds between the particles of which the nucleus is made. Some of this energy can be released, in the case of uranium (and a couple of other metals) by splitting the nucleus of the atom into two smaller nuclei. This can be done either slowly and for good purposes in a nuclear power station, or very rapidly in an atomic bomb.

Here are some other important types of energy. They are actually all different sorts of **kinetic energy**, but this is far from obvious in some cases:

If people just use the words 'kinetic energy', then they are referring to the energy of a visible moving object with k.e. = $\frac{1}{2}mv^2$.

'Internal energy'

This is contained within an object and makes the difference between the object being hot or cold. A hot object contains atoms that are moving fast or vibrating strongly.

'Electrical energy'

Electrical currents carry electrical energy from one place to another. 'Electrical energy' can easily be turned into kinetic energy in a motor or internal energy in a resistor, perhaps used as a heater.

'Light energy'

Light carries 'light energy' as it travels, and this will be turned into internal energy if it strikes most objects, but it can be made to generate 'electrical energy' if it hits a solar panel.

This cuckoo clock stores energy in two weights, one to run the mechanism that turns the hands, and one to make the cuckoo sing on each hour.

Sound waves

These carry a very small amount of energy from the source of the noise. (Do not confuse the 2000 W of electricity consumed by the rock group performing on stage, with the 100 W of sound being emitted by the loudspeakers. The ear is extremely good at detecting sound.)

CONVERSION OF ENERGY

We have already explained how kinetic energy and gravitational potential energy can be transferred backwards and forwards. In fact any type of energy can be transferred into any other type of energy. In some cases this transfer can be done efficiently, such as between kinetic energy and electrical energy. In other cases the transfer is inefficient, the most notorious example of this being the power station (see below).

In every case of transfer of energy, some of the energy is converted to internal energy. The light bulb creating light energy from electrical energy gets hot; the electric motor turning electrical energy to kinetic energy gets hot; the diesel engine using chemical energy gets hot; the battery that is being charged gets hot. Even the pendulum eventually stops swinging because the movement of the pendulum through the air heats up the air.

Conservation of energy

Don't confuse the words **conversion** and **conservation**.

Energy cannot be created or destroyed. You may need to describe how energy is transferred in different situations, but remember that total energy is always conserved: the energy at the start and at the end must have the same total value.

So you must account for all of the energy, and that includes the internal energy that will have been created, as well perhaps as light or sound.

For example, the streetcar takes electrical energy and converts it mainly into kinetic energy, but also into internal energy and sound.

Likewise, as the pendulum swings, some of its energy is transferred between kinetic and gravitational potential energy. But if you add up its total energy, you will find that the total stays almost the same. The oscillations of the pendulum slowly die away as energy is transferred to the air in the room and the air heats up slightly.

Efficiency of energy transfer

Energy transfers can be summarised using simple **energy transfer diagrams** or **Sankey diagrams**. The thickness of each arrow is drawn to scale to show the amount of energy.

Energy is always conserved – the total amount of energy after the transfer must be the same as the total amount of energy before the transfer. Unfortunately, in nearly all energy transfers some of the energy will end up as 'useless' heat.

In a power station only some of the energy originally produced from the fuel is transferred to useful electrical output. Energy **efficiency** can be calculated from the following formula:

$$\text{efficiency} = \frac{\text{useful energy output} \times 100\%}{\text{energy input}}$$

EXAMPLES

The electric motor that is used to power a train may take in 10 kW of electricity, and give out 9.5 kW of kinetic energy. From the formula you can calculate that the motor is 95% efficient. The other 5% of energy ends up increasing the temperature of the motor. This energy is wasted, and in fact the motor will need cooling fans to prevent it from overheating.

A diesel engine is more efficient than a petrol engine, and can give out 200 kW of kinetic energy while it is consuming diesel fuel at a rate of 500 kW. This is for an efficiency of 40%, which is a very good number for any process that uses heat. You will note that the engine will have to lose 300 kW of heat, much of it down the exhaust pipe, but it still needs a large radiator as well.

In a power station only some of the energy originally produced from the fuel is transferred to useful electrical output.

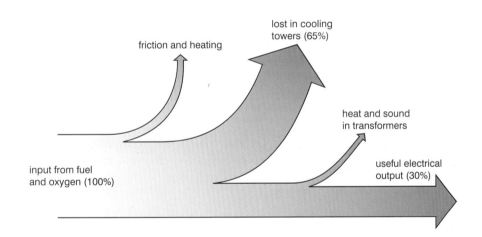

In a power station as much as 70% of the energy transfers do not produce useful energy. The power station is only 30% efficient.

Many power stations are now trying to make use of the large amounts of energy 'lost' in the hot water. In some cities, the houses of whole regions of the city are heated by hot water from the power station.

Scientists are working very hard to increase the efficiency of power stations. Some of the most recent power stations have had efficiencies nearer to 40%. This may not seem much at first sight, but if all power stations in the world could use a quarter less fuel, it would be a saving of millions of tonnes of coal or gas per year.

Conduction, convection and radiation

Energy will always try to flow from areas at high temperatures to areas at low temperatures. This is called **thermal transfer**. Thermal energy can be transferred in three main ways:

* **conduction**
* **convection**
* **radiation**.

CONDUCTION

Materials that allow thermal energy to transfer through them quickly are called **thermal conductors**. Those that do not are called **thermal insulators**. (If someone talks about an 'insulator', you may have to work out for yourself if he is referring to a thermal insulator or to an electrical insulator.)

If one end of a conductor is heated, the atoms that make up its structure start to vibrate more vigorously. As the atoms in a solid are linked together by chemical bonds, the increased vibration can be passed on to other atoms. The energy of movement (kinetic energy) passes through the whole material.

Conduction in a solid. Particles in a hot part of a solid (top) vibrate further and faster than particles in a cold part (bottom). The vibrations are passed on through the bonds from particle to particle.

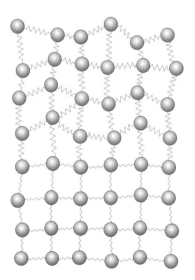

Metals are particularly good thermal conductors because they contain freely moving electrons which transfer energy very rapidly. As the electrons travel all over the piece of metal, they take the thermal energy with them. This is in addition to the thermal energy that is transferred by vibrations of the atoms that make up the structure of the metal.

Conduction cannot occur when there are no particles present, so a vacuum is a perfect insulator.

In this experiment to show conduction, the rods are made of different metals, so the heat conducts along them at different rates. The better the conductor, the quicker the wax at the end of the rod melts.

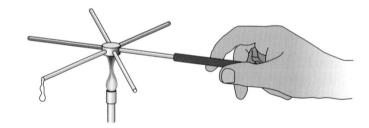

CONVECTION

Convection occurs in **liquids** and **gases** because these materials flow (they are 'fluids'). The particles in a fluid move all the time. When a fluid is heated, energy is transferred to the particles, causing them to move faster and further apart. This makes the heated fluid less dense than the unheated fluid. The less dense warm fluid will rise above the more dense colder fluid, causing the fluid to circulate. This **convection current** is how the thermal energy is transferred.

If a fluid's movement is restricted, then energy cannot be transferred. That is why many insulators, such as ceiling tiles, contain trapped air pockets. Wall cavities in houses are filled with fibre to prevent air from circulating and transferring thermal energy by convection.

Potassium permanganate crystals in water demonstrate convection. The warmer water expands, becomes less dense and rises, making a trail as some of the dissolved potassium permanganate is carried along as well.

RADIATION

Radiation, unlike conduction and convection, **does not need particles** at all. Radiation can travel through a vacuum. This is clearly shown by the radiation that arrives from the Sun. Radiated heat energy is carried mainly by infrared radiation, which is part of the electromagnetic spectrum.

All objects take in and give out infrared radiation all the time. Hot objects radiate more infrared than cold objects. The amount of radiation given out or absorbed by an object depends on its temperature and on its surface.

Type of surface	As an emitter of radiation	As an absorber of radiation	Examples
Dull black	Good	Good	Emitter: Cooling fins on the back of a refrigerator are dull black to radiate away more energy. Absorber: The surface of a black bitumen road gets far hotter on a sunny day than the surface of a white concrete one.
Bright shiny	Poor	Poor	Emitter: Marathon runners, at the end of a race, wrap themselves in shiny blankets to prevent them from cooling down too quickly by radiation (or convection). Absorber: Fuel storage tanks are sprayed with shiny silver or white paint to reflect radiation from the Sun.

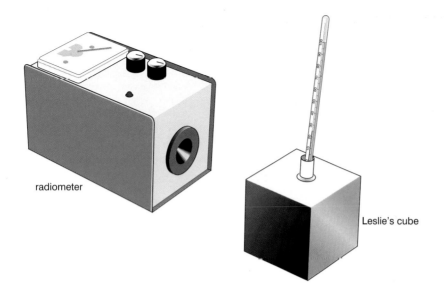

radiometer

Leslie's cube

Leslie's cube has sides with different surfaces – shiny, dull, dark, light – to show how they emit and absorb thermal radiation at different rates. Because all sides of the cube are heated by the same water inside the cube, any differences in the way they radiate energy can only be due to the differences in their surfaces.

Everyday examples of thermal transfer

A radiator does radiate some heat, and if you stand near a hot radiator your hands can feel the infrared radiation being emitted by the front surface of the radiator. However, this is only around one quarter of the heat being released by the radiator. *Three quarters* of the heat is taken away by the hot air that rises from the radiator. Colder air from the room flows in to replace this hot air, and a convection current is formed as shown.

This shows a side view of a room with a hot-water radiator underneath the window.

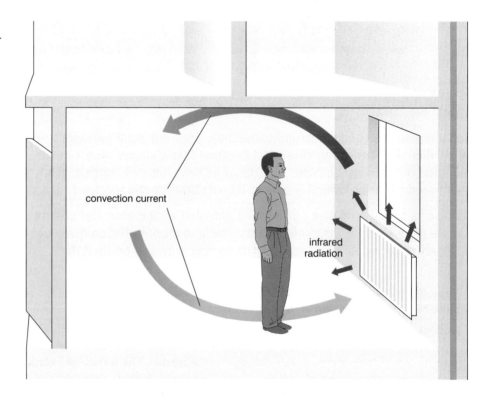

convection current

infrared radiation

You will note that the convection current is far more efficient at heating the top of the room than it is at heating the person standing in front of the radiator.

The vacuum flask will keep a drink hot or cold for hours by almost completely eliminating the flow of heat out or in.

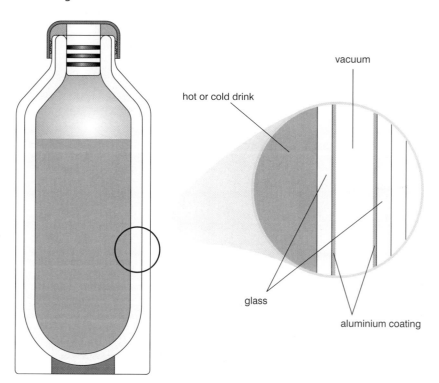

Conduction is almost eliminated by making sure that any heat flowing out must travel along the glass of the neck of the flask. The path is a long one, the glass is thin, and glass is a very poor conductor of heat. The bung in the top of the flask must also be a very poor conductor of heat: cork or expanded polystyrene is good.

Convection is eliminated because the space between the inner wall and the outer wall of the flask is made a vacuum so that there is no air to form convection currents.

If the contents are hot, radiation is almost eliminated because the inner walls of the flask are coated with pure aluminium. Because the aluminium is in a vacuum, it stays extremely shiny forever, and so the wall in contact with the hot liquid emits very little infrared radiation.

Conduction plays an important part in cooking food.

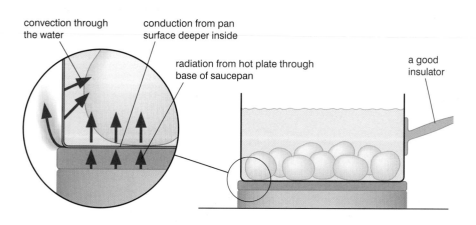

Using insulation to reduce energy transfers

There are a number of ways of reducing wasteful energy transfers in a house. The diagram below shows some of them.

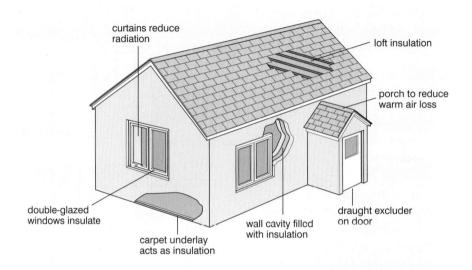

Source of energy wastage	% of energy wasted	Insulation technique
Walls	35	*Cavity wall insulation.* Modern houses have cavity walls, that is, two single walls separated by an air cavity. The air reduces energy transfer by conduction but not by convection as the air is free to move within the cavity. Fibre insulation is inserted into the cavity to prevent the air from moving and so reduces convection.
Roof	25	*Loft insulation.* Fibre insulation is placed on top of the ceiling and between the wooden joists. Air is trapped between the fibres, reducing energy transfer by conduction and convection.
Floors	15	*Carpets.* Carpets and underlay prevent energy loss by conduction and convection. In some modern houses foam blocks are placed under the floors.
Draughts	15	*Draught excluders.* Cold air can get into the home through gaps between windows and doors and their frames. Draught excluder tape can be used to block these gaps.
Windows	10	*Double glazing.* Energy is transferred through glass by conduction and radiation. Double glazing has two panes of glass with a layer of air between the panes. It reduces energy transfer by conduction but not by radiation. Radiation can be reduced by drawing the curtains.

Mountaineers and other people who need clothing to protect them from extreme cold know that they need to wear several layers of clothing, with each layer full of trapped air. The whole aim is to have a thick layer of air around the body, because air is a poor conductor of heat.

The fibres of clothes, especially the newer extremely fine spun-polyester Polartec™ fibres, do a very good job at stopping the air from moving, thus preventing convection. Mountaineers do not use metallised layers to prevent radiation, because such layers would trap perspiration and could hamper movement. However, metallised plastic layers are used in the emergency survival bags that mountaineers carry in case of accident.

REVIEW QUESTIONS

Q1 Why are several thin layers of clothing more likely to reduce thermal transfer than one thick layer of clothing?

Q2 The diagram shows a cross-section of a steel radiator positioned in a room next to a wall.

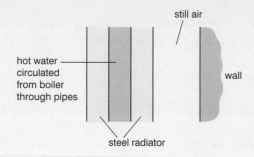

still air

hot water circulated from boiler through pipes

wall

steel radiator

Describe how energy from the hot water reaches the wall behind the radiator.

More questions on the CD ROM

WORK AND POWER

Work

Work is done when the application of a force results in movement. Work can only be done if the object or system has energy. When work is done energy is transferred.

Work done is equal to the amount of energy transferred. It can be calculated using the following formula:

work done = force × distance moved = energy transferred

$W = F \times d = E$

> W = work done in joules (J)
>
> F = force in newtons (N)
>
> d = distance moved in the direction of the force in metres (m)
>
> E = energy transferred in joules (J)

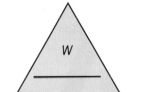

WORKED EXAMPLES

1 A cyclist pedals along a flat road. She exerts a force of 60 N and travels 150 m. Calculate the work done by the cyclist.

Write down the formula:	$W = F \times d$
Substitute the values for F and d:	$W = 60 \times 150$
Work out the answer and write down the unit:	$W = 9000$ J

2 A person does 3000 J of work in pushing a supermarket trolley 50 m across a level car park. What force was the person exerting on the trolley?

Write down the formula with F as the subject:	$F = \dfrac{W}{d}$
Substitute the values for W and d:	$F = \dfrac{3000}{50}$
Work out the answer and write down the unit:	$F = 60$ N

In this position the gymnast is not doing any work against his body weight – he is not moving (he will be doing work pumping blood around his body though).

The gymnast is doing work. He is moving upwards against the force of gravity. Energy is being transferred as he does the work.

Gravitational potential energy and kinetic energy

If a load is raised above the ground, it will have **gravitational potential energy (G.P.E.)**. If the load moves back to the ground, the stored potential energy is transferred to movement energy, which is called **kinetic energy** (K.E.).

Gravitational potential energy can be calculated using the formula:

gravitational potential energy = mass × gravitational field strength × height

$$G.P.E. = m\,g\,h$$

G.P.E. = gravitational potential energy in joules (J)

m = mass in kilograms (kg)

g = gravitational field strength of 10 N/kg

h = height in metres (m)

A* EXTRA

An object gains gravitational potential energy as it gains height. Work has to be done to increase the height of the object above the ground. Therefore:

> gain in gravitational potential energy of an object = work done on that object against gravity.

WORKED EXAMPLE

A skier has a mass of 70 kg and travels up a ski lift a vertical height of 300 m. Calculate the change in the skier's gravitational potential energy.

Write down the formula:	G.P.E. = $m\,g\,h$
Substitute values for m, g and h:	G.P.E. = $70 \times 10 \times 300$
Work out the answer and write down the unit:	G.P.E. = 210 000 J or 210 kJ

The kinetic energy of an object depends on its mass and its velocity. The kinetic energy can be calculated using the following formula:

kinetic energy = $\frac{1}{2}$ × mass × velocity^2

$$K.E. = \frac{1}{2}mv^2$$

K.E. = kinetic energy in joules (J)

m = mass in kilograms (kg)

v = velocity in m/s

WORKED EXAMPLE

An ice-skater has a mass of 50 kg and travels at a velocity of 5 m/s. Calculate the ice-skater's kinetic energy.

Write down the formula:	K.E. = $\frac{1}{2}mv^2$
Substitute the values for m and v:	K.E. = $\frac{1}{2} \times 50 \times 5 \times 5$
Work out the answer and write down the unit:	K.E. = 625 J

A* EXTRA

As a skier skis down a mountain the loss in potential energy should equal the gain in kinetic energy (assuming no other energy transfers take place, as a result of friction, for example). Calculations can then be performed using:

> loss in G.P.E. = gain in K.E.
> ($mgh = \frac{1}{2}mv^2$)

The kinetic energy given to the stone when it is thrown is transferred to potential energy as it gains height and slows down. At the top of its flight a large part of the kinetic energy will have been converted into gravitational potential energy. A small amount of energy will have been lost due to friction between the stone and the air.

A* EXTRA

Note that in this worked example, the answer has been given to four significant figures. In most physics examples at this level, you should remember to use three or four significant figures, not the ten or more digits that your calculator might give! You may be penalised in an exam if you give too many.

Energy at work

You can use the principle of the conservation of energy to calculate what happens when kinetic energy and potential energy are converted from either one to the other.

So long as negligible energy is lost in the conversion, $mgh = \frac{1}{2}mv^2$.

WORKED EXAMPLE

If a stone thrown vertically upwards reaches a height of 6 m above the hand of the thrower, with what speed was it thrown?

The decrease in K.E. of the stone as it rises equals the increase in the G.P.E. of the stone.

As the final K.E. of the stone is 0, the initial K.E. of the stone equals the increase in the G.P.E. of the stone at the top of its flight.

Write down the formula:	$\frac{1}{2}mv^2 = mgh$
Note that the mass has cancelled out because the mass does not matter in this case.	$\frac{1}{2}v^2 = gh$
Substitute values for g and h:	$v^2 = gh \times 2$
	$= 10 \times 6 \times 2$
	$= 120$
Work out the answer and write down the unit:	$v = \sqrt{120}$
	$= 10.95$ m/s

Power

A powerful engine in a car can take you up a road to the top of a mountain more quickly than a less-powerful engine. Both engines can do the work, given enough time, but the powerful engine can do the work more quickly. In the same way, a powerful electric motor on a cooling fan will move the air in the room more quickly; and the 'powerfully built' athlete will, by transferring more kinetic energy to it as it is launched, throw the javelin further.

Power is defined as the rate of doing work or the rate of transferring energy. The more powerful a machine is, the quicker it does a fixed amount of work or transfers a fixed amount of energy.

Power can be calculated using the formula:

$$\text{power} = \frac{\text{work done}}{\text{time taken}} = \frac{\text{energy transferred}}{\text{time taken}}$$

$$P = \frac{W}{t} \text{ or } P = \frac{E}{t}$$

P = power in joules per second or watts (W)

E = energy transferred in joules (J)

W = work done in joules (J)

t = time taken in seconds (s)

WORKED EXAMPLES

1 A crane lifts a 100 kg girder for a skyscraper by 20 m in 40 s. Hence it does 20 000 J of work in 40 seconds. Calculate its power over this time. Note: this calculation tells you the size of electric motor that the crane needs.

Write down the formula:	$P = \dfrac{W}{t}$
Substitute the values for W and t:	$P = \dfrac{20\,000}{40}$
Work out the answer and write down the unit:	$P = 500\,\text{W}$

2 A student with a weight of 600 N runs up the flight of stairs shown in the diagram (right) in 6 seconds. Calculate the student's power.

Write down the formula for work done:	$W = F\,d$
Substitute the values for F and d:	$W = 600 \times 5 = 3000\,\text{J}$
Write down the formula for power:	$P = \dfrac{W}{t}$
Substitute the values for W and t:	$P = \dfrac{3000}{6}$
Work out the answer and write down the unit	$P = 500\,\text{W}$

5m

The student is lifting his body against the force of gravity, which acts in a vertical direction. The distance measured must be in the direction of the force (that is, the vertical height).

REVIEW QUESTIONS

Q1 50 000 J of work are done as a crane lifts a load of 400 kg. How far did the crane lift the load? (Gravitational field strength, g, is 10 N/kg.)

Q2 A student is carrying out a personal fitness test.
She steps on and off the 'step' 200 times.
She transfers 90 J of energy each time she steps up.
a Calculate the energy transferred during the test.
b She takes 3 minutes to do the test. Calculate her average power.

Q3 A child of mass 35 kg climbed a 30 m high snow-covered hill.
a Calculate the change in the child's gravitational potential energy.
b The child then climbed onto a lightweight sledge and slid down the hill. Calculate the child's maximum speed at the bottom of the hill. (Ignore the mass of the sledge.)
c Explain why the actual speed at the bottom of the hill is likely to be less than the value calculated in part b.

More questions on the CD ROM

ENERGY RESOURCES AND ELECTRICITY GENERATION

Most of the energy we use is obtained from **fossil fuels** – coal, oil and natural gas.

Once supplies of these fuels have been used up. they cannot be replaced – they are **non-renewable**.

At current levels of use, oil and gas supplies will last for about another 40 years, and coal supplies for about a further 300 years. The development of **renewable** sources of energy is therefore becoming increasingly important.

The **wind** is used to turn windmill-like turbines which generate electricity directly from the rotating motion of their blades. Modern wind turbines are very efficient but several thousand would be required to equal the generating capacity of a modern fossil-fuel power station.

The motion of **waves** can be used to move large floats and generate electricity. A very large number of floats are needed to produce a significant amount of electricity.

Dams on tidal estuaries trap the water at high tide. When the water is allowed to flow back at low tide, **tidal power** can be generated. This obviously limits the use of the estuary.

On a windy day this wind turbine generates 2000 kW of electricity. That's enough for 1200 families.

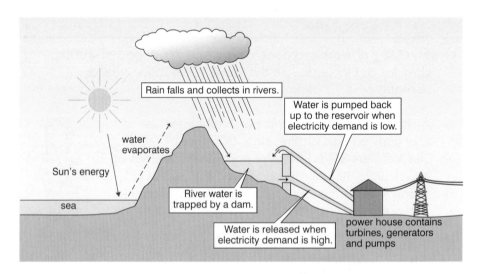

Rain falls and collects in rivers.

Water is pumped back up to the reservoir when electricity demand is low.

water evaporates

Sun's energy

sea

River water is trapped by a dam.

Water is released when electricity demand is high.

power house contains turbines, generators and pumps

A 'pumped storage' hydroelectric power station.

Dams can be used to store **water** which is allowed to fall in a controlled way that generates electricity. This is particularly useful in mountainous regions for generating **hydroelectric power**. When demand for electricity is low, electricity can be used to pump water back up into the high dam for use in times of high demand.

Plants use energy from the Sun in photosynthesis. Plant material can then be used as a **biomass fuel** – either directly by burning it or indirectly. A good example of indirect use is to ferment sugar cane to make ethanol, which is then used as an alternative to petrol. Waste plant material can be used in 'biodigesters' to produce methane gas. The methane is then used as a fuel.

Geothermal power is obtained using the heat of the Earth. In certain parts of the world, water forms hot springs which can be used directly for heating. Water can also be pumped deep into the ground to be heated.

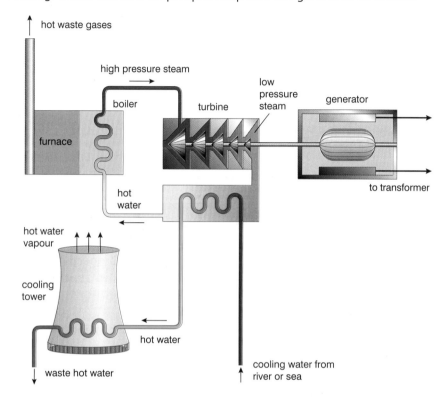

The most common fuels used in power stations are still coal, oil and gas.

This nuclear power station produces 3 m^3 of waste per year. People disagree over whether this radioactive waste is more hazardous than the gases emitted by the 4 million tonnes of coal burned by a single coal power station each year.

REVIEW QUESTIONS

Q1 **a** What is meant by a non-renewable energy source?
b Name three non-renewable energy sources.
c Which non-renewable energy source is likely to last the longest?

Q2 Look at the graph, which shows the amount of energy from different sources used in the OECD nations between 1980 and 2001.

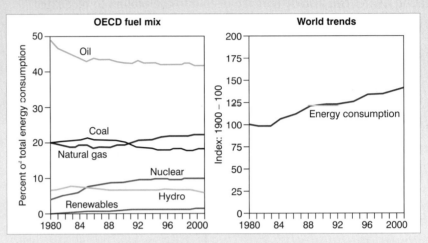

a Describe the trend in the total energy used in this period.
b Describe the main changes in the sources of this energy.
c What do you expect to happen to these graphs in the next 20 years? Give reasons where possible.

Q3 A site has been chosen for a wind farm (a series of windmill-like turbines).
a Give two important factors in choosing the site.
b Give one advantage and one disadvantage of using wind farms to generate electricity.

More questions on the CD ROM

Many plants, such as the cactus, have very few leaves, which reduces the surface area and so less particles of water can evaporate. Desert plants often have very long roots. These allow the plant to store the water it has as deep as possible, thus reducing the chances of the water particles being lost as water vapour

Collection of succulents including: Blue Echeveria, Panda Plant, Haworthia Cymbiformis

Surviving the desert

What makes a desert? A place that is very hot? No, the key feature that defines a desert is a place that is very dry. This might be because the area is close to the equator and so receives the most heating from the Sun, or it could be because local mountain ranges cause rain to fall elsewhere, leaving a dry desert area.

If a plant or animal is going to survive in a desert area, particularly a hot desert area, it is going to need to be very careful about keeping and using water. High temperatures will cause any available water to evaporate as some particles will have enough energy to leave the liquid. The lack of water means that temperatures often fall very quickly at night. This is because invisible water vapour in the air usually reflects the heat back down and so acts as a blanket to keep the ground warm, but above a desert there is less water, and so it gets cold. Clouds also act as blankets, and deserts tend not to have these either.

SOLIDS, LIQUIDS AND GASES

Molecular graphic of
evaporating
water molcules

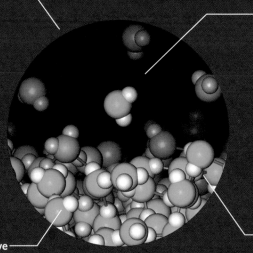

As the temperature of water increases, more
and more molecules on the surface of the
water have enough thermal energy to break the
hydrogen bonds, and so evaporate to form a
vapour. The evaporation becomes rapid as the
temperature approaches 100°C, and when the
temperature reaches 100°C, at sea level, the
water boils

Water molecules have
one oxygen atom (light blue)
and two hydrogen atoms
(white)

Each molecule is neutral, but the oxygen has a small
negative charge and the hydrogens are slightly positive.
The hydrogens are attracted to oxygens in nearby
molecules, forming weak hydrogen bonds (dark blue)

DENSITY AND PRESSURE

Gold is one of the densest metals. A block the size of a 1 L carton of milk would have a mass of almost 20 kg and would be very hard to pick up.

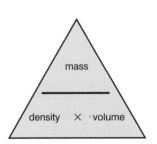

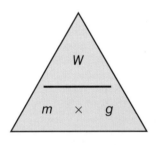

Density

We must have all noticed that the weight of objects can vary greatly. A plastic teaspoon weighs less than a metal one, and a gold ring weighs twice as much as a silver one, even if the objects are exactly the same size.

The density of a material is a measure of how 'squashed up' it is, and a heavy object contains more mass than a light object of the same size.

Density is calculated using this formula:

$$\text{density} = \frac{\text{mass}}{\text{volume}}$$

$$\rho = \frac{m}{V}$$

m = mass in g or kg

V = volume in cm^3 or m^3

ρ = density in g/cm^3 or kg/m^3

Note that in this equation you must use g and cm throughout or you must use kg and m. And note that if you measure the weight in N you must convert it into g or kg.

THE DENSITY OF A REGULARLY SHAPED OBJECT

WORKED EXAMPLE

The brick has dimensions 20 cm × 9 cm × 6.5 cm.
Weight of brick = 22.2 N
What is the density of the brick?

Mass of brick:

$$m = \frac{W}{g}$$

$$= \frac{22.2}{10}$$

$$= 2.2 \text{ kg or } 2220 \text{ g}$$

(Remember that 1 kg = 1000 g)

Volume of brick:

$$V = 20 \times 9 \times 6.5$$

$$= 1170 \text{ cm}^3$$

Density of brick:

$$\rho = \frac{\text{mass}}{\text{volume}}$$

$$= \frac{2220}{1170}$$

$$= 1.90 \text{ g/cm}^3$$

Note that the density of water is 1.0 g/cm^3, and the rule is that an object of greater density will sink in a liquid of lower density. So, perhaps not surprisingly, the brick will sink in water. But will it sink in mercury? See the table right.

Some useful densities

	Density in g/cm³	Density in kg/m³
Vacuum	0	0
Helium gas	0.00017	0.17
Air	0.00124	1.24
Oil (Petroleum)	0.88	880
Water	1.0	1000
Sea water	1.03	1030
Plastic	0.9 – 1.6	900 – 1600
Wood	0.5 – 1.3	500 – 1300
Magnesium	1.74	1740
Aluminium	2.7	2700
Titanium	4.5	4500
Steel	7.8	7800
Mercury (liquid)	13.6	13600
Silver	10.5	10500
Gold	19.3	19300

WHY DO MATERIALS HAVE DIFFERENT DENSITIES?

If you look inside a block of gold and inside a block of aluminium with a modern electron microscope, you will see that the atoms are almost exactly the same size (the gold atoms are just a little bit bigger). As we will see later, most of an atom is actually empty space, and the mass of an atom is concentrated in the nucleus, which is far smaller than the atom. So the extra density of the gold is due to the fact that the nuclei of the gold atoms are far more massive than the nuclei of the aluminium ones.

Many materials have a lower density because they contain large bubbles or other voids inside them. Bread has a lower density than most cakes; and expanded polystyrene cups have a lower density than other cups.

A bag of popcorn has a far lower density than the same bag filled with corn that has not been popped.

The choice of materials used to make an aircraft is critical in making it as light as possible and thus reducing fuel consumption.

An airplane is another example of a lower density. Although airplanes are made of aluminium and other light metals, there is no way that an airplane could fly if it was made of solid aluminum. In fact the average densities of all airplanes is sufficiently low that, in the event of a forced landing on water, they can easily float for long enough for everyone to escape.

WORKED EXAMPLE

What is the mass of a block of expanded polystyrene that is 1 m long, 0.5 m wide and 0.3 m high? The density of this sample of expanded polystyrene is 40 kg/m^3.

Volume of block:	$V = 1.0 \times 0.5 \times 0.3$
	$= 0.15 \text{ m}^3$
Write down the formula:	$m = \rho \times V$
Substitue the values for ρ and V:	$m = 40 \times 0.15$
Work out the answer and write down the units:	$m = 6 \text{ kg}$

Measuring the density of an irregular object

This method only works if the object is denser than the liquid used so that it sinks. It does not work if the object absorbs the liquid, nor if it is damaged by the liquid.

Step 1

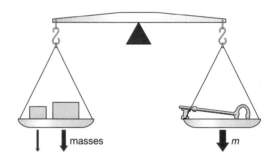

Use a balance to weigh the object in question and so find its mass, m.

Step 2

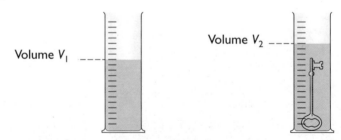

Choose a measuring cylinder that will accept the object. A narrower cylinder will give a more accurate answer than a wider one. Add liquid to the cylinder to fill it to a deep enough level so that the object will be completely submerged, and then measure the volume of liquid V_1. The exact amount of liquid that you use is not at all critical. Water is often the liquid used.

Step 3

Lower the object into the liquid (without splashing) and measure the new reading V_2. This is the volume of the object and the liquid. The volume of the object is $V_2 - V_1$.

From the mass and the volume you can calculate the density of the object.

WORKED EXAMPLE

A small metal statue is measured to have a mass of 90 g.
A measuring cylinder is filled with water to the 82 cm³ mark. The statue is lowered into the measuring cylinder and the water rises to the 91 cm³ mark. What is the statue made of?

Volume of the statue: $V = 91 - 82$

$= 9$ cm³

Write down the formula: $\rho = \dfrac{m}{V}$

Substitute the values for m and V: $\rho = \dfrac{90}{9}$

Work out the answer and write down the units: $\rho = 10$ g/cm³

So from the table on page 99, the statue is made of, what?

Of course an experiment of this type is never perfectly accurate, so the density that we measure will never be exactly the same as the official values.

Pressure

The snowmobile in the picture can travel over soft snow because its weight is spread by the skis over a large area of snow. If the rider got off and stood on the snow, he would probably sink into it up to his knees, even though he is much lighter than the snowmobile.

If a pair of shoes has small heels, the wearer can easily damage a wooden floor by sinking into it. And a drawing pin is pushed into a notice board by the pressure of your thumb.

In every case the question is not just what force is used, but also what area it is spread over. Where we have a large force over a small area, we have a high pressure, and a small force over a large area gives us a low pressure.

Pressure is measured in newtons per square metre (N/m^2), but note that it is often given the special name of pascal (Pa). So 1 Pa = 1 N/m^2.

In order to measure how 'spread out' a force is, use this formula:

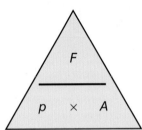

$$\text{pressure} = \frac{\text{force}}{\text{area}}$$

$$p = \frac{F}{A}$$

p = pressure in pascals, Pa
(or newtons per square metre, N/m^2)

F = force in newtons, N

A = area in m^2

WORKED EXAMPLE

What pressure on the snow does the snowmobile make if it has a weight of 800 N and the runners have an area of 0.2 m^2?

Write down the formula:	$p = \frac{F}{A}$
Confirm that F is in N and A is in m^2.	
Substitute the values for F and A:	$p = \frac{800}{0.2}$
Work out the answer and write down the units:	p = 4000Pa or 4 kPa

Note that 4 kPa is a very low pressure. If you stand on the ground in basketball shoes, the pressure on the ground will be around 20 kPa. The wheel of a car generates a pressure on the ground of around 200 kPa. Pressures can be quite high, and so the kPa is often used.

Pressure in fluids

Because particles in a liquid or gas (i.e. in fluids) are constantly in random motion, they are constantly colliding with each other and the walls of the container. This causes a force on the other particles and the container walls. Usually we describe this force in terms of the pressure it causes on a particular area.

ATMOSPHERIC PRESSURE

Because we have spent all of our lives living in the atmosphere of the Earth, we seldom think that we have 20 km or so of air pressing on us. We do not feel the pressure because it does not just push down, it pushes us inwards from all sides. Our lungs do not collapse, because the same air pressure flows into our lungs and presses outwards. It would be a very different story if our lungs did not contain any air and there was a vacuum inside them.

We can show this by seeing how a plastic bottle collapses if the air is removed from it.

The plastic bottle is filled with steam from a kettle so that the air in it is replaced by the steam. The lid is screwed onto the bottle, and the bottle is cooled by immersing it in cold water. When the steam turns back into water, the bottle collapses due to the pressure of the air outside.

Warning: steam from a kettle is extremely dangerous, and much more so than boiling water. You must never put your hands near the steam coming out of a boiling kettle, and you must not perform this experiment without suitable safety equipment and training.

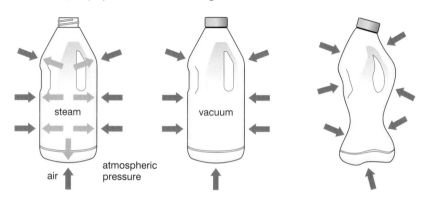

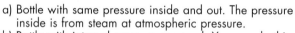

a) Bottle with same pressure inside and out. The pressure inside is from steam at atmospheric pressure.
b) Bottle with internal pressure removed. You can do this with a strong metal bottle, but not with a plastic one.
c) Plastic bottle collapsed.

Atmospheric pressure is approximately 100 kPa. This value is a pure coincidence. In fact it is around 101.3 kPa, though it increases and decreases by 5 per cent or so depending on the weather. But in the same way that we often take g to be 10 m/s^2 on the Earth when it is more accurately 9.8 m/s^2, we often choose to take atmospheric pressure to be 100 kPa.

Pressure is also measured in bar and millibar. Normal atmospheric pressure is approximately 1 bar. The pressure on a scuba diver's cylinder of air can easily be 200 bar. You will see millibar used in some weather forecasts. Atmospheric pressure is approximately 1000 mbar.

THE MERCURY BAROMETER

The mercury barometer is made of a glass tube, sealed at the top. It contains mercury, and the base of the tube dips into a beaker, and below the surface of the mercury in the beaker.

Atmospheric pressure pushes down on the mercury in the beaker, which in turn pushes mercury up the tube.

If the space above the mercury in the tube is a vacuum, then nothing is pushing down on the top of the mercury in the tube, and atmospheric pressure will push the mercury up until the weight of the column of mercury balances the atmospheric pressure. The height h from the top of the mercury in the beaker to the top of the mercury in the tube can be used to calculate atmospheric pressure.

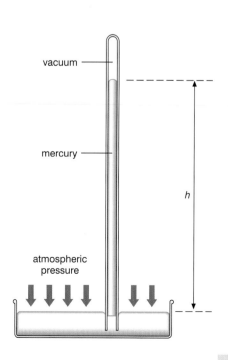

This height *h* is approximately 760 mm of mercury, and in some countries atmospheric pressure is still quoted in mm of mercury.

Note that mercury has a convex (curved-upwards) shape when in contact with glass. You should measure to the top of the mercury in the tube, and to the flat surface of the mercury in the beaker.

Mercury barometers are no longer made because mercury is a highly poisonous metal with a poisonous vapour.

Pressure difference, height and density

If you dive below the water, the height of the water above you also puts pressure on you. At a depth of 10 m of water, the pressure has increased by 100 kPa, and for each further 10 m of depth the pressure increases by another 100 kPa. The rapid increase in pressure explains why scuba divers cannot go down more than 20 m without great difficulty.

The hull of a submarine is made very strong so that the submariners can breathe air at the normal pressure.

The increase in pressure below the surface of a liquid depends on (a) the depth below the surface and (b) the density of the liquid. So the pressure will be much higher at a certain depth below the surface of mercury than it is below the surface of water. It does not depend on anything else, and note in particular that the pressure does not depend on the width of the water. If a diver goes to inspect a well, the pressure 10 m below the surface is the same as the pressure 10 m below the surface of a large lake. This explains why an engineer who is designing a dam needs to make it the same thickness whether the lake that will be made is going to be 100 m long or 100 km long.

These scuba divers breathe compressed air at high pressure to prevent their lungs collapsing due to the high pressure from the water above them. This is a safe sport, but only because novices are trained to a very high standard.

The pressure on the diver is the same in the well and in the lake. In both cases it depends only on the density of the liquid and his depth, *h*.

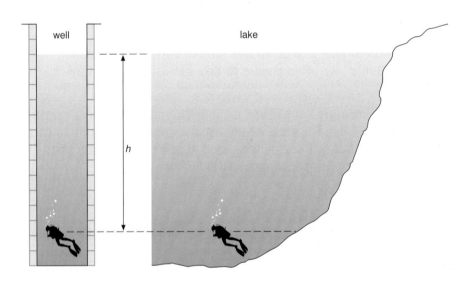

The pressure below the surface of a fluid, and in fact between any two points in the fluid can be calculated by the following equation:

pressure difference = height × density × strength of the gravitational field

$$p = h \times \rho \times g$$

p = pressure difference in pascals (Pa)

ρ = density in kilograms per cubic metre (kg/m³)

g = acceleration of free fall (m/s²)

Note that the density ρ must be in kg/m³. If it is quoted in g/cm³, you must convert it. Remember that 1 g/cm³ = 1000 kg/m³.

Note that there is one major cause of confusion. Consider the pressure on a scuba diver. Before he jumps in, the pressure on him is already 100 kPa (or 1 bar). When he has dived down 10 m, the pressure on him increases by 100 kPa, so the total pressure on him is now 200 kPa (2 bar). The pressure is coming 100 kPa from the air above him, and 100 kPa from the water above him. At 20 m, the total pressure on him is 300 kPa, and so on.

WORKED EXAMPLE

An aquarium has a tunnel through a tank of water at a depth of 5 m below the surface. The manufacturer guarantees the tunnel to a pressure difference of 200 kPa. Is the tunnel safe?

Write down the equation: $p = h \times \rho \times g$

Substitute the values into the equation: $p = 5 \times 1000 \times 10$

Work out the answer and write down the unit: $p = 50\ 000$ Pa or 50 kPa

The tunnel is safe.

Note that the total pressure on the outside of the tunnel is 50 kPa from the water, plus 100 kPa from the air pushing on top of the water, giving 150 kPa. However, the tunnel is also full of air, which is pushing outwards with a pressure of 100 kPa. So the tunnel only has to stand a pressure difference of 50 kPa.

THE MANOMETER

Manometers are used to measure the pressure difference between two regions. They are used, for example, on cleanrooms where computer chips and other semiconductor devices are made. It is necessary to ensure that the pressure inside the room is slightly higher than outside in order to prevent dust finding its way into the cleanroom through small gaps in the wall.

A manometer is mounted on the wall of the cleanroom. It consists of a tube of plastic or glass, bent into the U-shape shown, and filled with a liquid that is often oil. If there is a pressure difference between the ends of the manometer, the liquid moves until the pressure difference is balanced by the *difference* in height of the ends of the liquid. The greater the pressure, the greater the difference in height. You will note immediately that the liquid will be blown out if the pressure difference is too great.

A manometer.

Oil is used rather than water because water evaporates and also because oil, being lighter, makes the manometer more sensitive: for the same pressure difference, the oil will move further.

The pressure difference between the two regions is given by the following equation:

$$\Delta p = h\rho g$$

This is basically the same equation as $p = h \times \rho \times g$.

WORKED EXAMPLE

The manometer on an industrial machine shows that the oil is being sucked towards the machine and the height difference, h is 20 cm. What is the pressure inside the machine if the pressure outside is 100 kPa? The oil has a density of 800 kg/m^3.

Write down the equation:	$\Delta p = h\rho g$
Be sure to convert the height h into m:	20 cm = 0.2 m
Substitute the values into the equation:	$\Delta p = 0.2 \times 800 \times 10$
Work out the answer and write down the unit:	$\Delta p = 1600$ Pa or 1.6 kPa

The pressure inside the machine must be lower than atmospheric pressure. Therefore the pressure inside the machine is (100 − 1.6) kPa

= 98.4 kPa

REVIEW QUESTIONS

Q1 Which of the following objects will sink?
- wood in oil
- wood in mercury
- plastic in oil
- steel in mercury
- silver in air
- gold in mercury (this experiment must be done rapidly as the gold will dissolve very quickly)
- helium balloon in air

The answer may be that 'It depends on what sample of the material you choose'.

Q2 Write out the worked example on page 98 for the case of the student who measures all the lengths of the brick in m, and calculates with the mass in kg. Give the answer in kg/m^3.

Q3 A king believes that his jeweller has given him a crown that is a mixture of gold and silver, and not the 1.93 kg of pure gold that he paid for. He weighs the crown in a balance and finds that it has the correct mass of 1.93 kg. He then immerses it in a measuring jug where the water level was 800 cm^3. If the crown is pure gold, what will the new water level be? What will happen to the water level if the jeweller has cheated?

Q4 Calculate the pressure generated by an ordinary shoe heel (person of mass 40 kg, heel 5 cm × 5 cm), an elephant (of mass 500 kg, foot of 20 cm diameter) and a high-heeled shoe (person of mass 40 kg, heel of area 0.5 cm^2). Which ones will damage a wooden floor that starts to yield at a pressure of 4000 kPa?

Note that to convert from cm^2 to m^2 you need to divide by 10 000.

Q5 The pressure gauge on a submarine in a river was reading 100 kPa when it was at the surface. If a sailor notices that the gauge is now reading 250 kPa, how deep is he? How would the answer change if he were diving in sea water that is slightly denser than fresh water?

Q6 A diver on Saturn's moon Titan is 50 m below the surface of a lake of liquid methane. What is the increase in pressure on him due to his depth in the methane? The density of liquid methane is 0.42 g/cm^3. The acceleration of gravity on Titan is 1.4 m/s^2.

We are told that the pressure of the atmosphere on Titan is 1600 mbar. What is the total pressure on the diver (in kPa)?

More questions on the CD ROM

CHANGE OF STATE

The main body of this rocket is filled with liquid oxygen and liquid hydrogen, which have to be kept at extremely low temperatures to prevent them from heating up and turning back into gas. If the fuel were made colder it would turn into a solid.

The molten iron can be poured into a mould before it cools down and turns back into a solid.

States of matter

Almost all matter can be classified as a solid, a liquid or a gas. These are called the **three states of matter**.

(The fourth state of matter is called 'plasma'. It only exists at high temperatures seldom seen on Earth, and so we won't consider it further here, even though most of the matter in the universe and most stars are made of plasma.)

As you will know, in general solids can be turned into liquids by heating, and with more heating liquids can be turned into gas. We are all familiar with water in all three states, but less so with other materials. Solid air is uncommon simply because it only exists at extremely low temperatures, and iron in the form of a gas only exists at very high temperatures.

We now know that all materials are made of tiny particles called **atoms**. The atoms attract each other, and the particles in a solid are locked together by the forces between them. But even in a solid the particles are not completely still. They vibrate constantly about their fixed positions. If the material is heated, it is given more internal energy, and the particles vibrate faster and further.

If the temperature is increased more, the vibrations of the particles increase to the point where the forces are no longer strong enough to hold the structure together. The forces are no longer enough to prevent the atoms moving around, but they do prevent the atoms from flying apart from each other. This gives us a liquid. The volume of the liquid is the volume occupied by the volume of the particles of which it is made.

If the temperature is increased even more, then the particles do indeed fly apart. They now form a gas. The particles fly around at high speed (several hundred kilometres per hour) and if they are in a container, they travel all over the container, bouncing off the walls. The volume of a gas is not fixed, it just depends on the size of the container that the gas is put in.

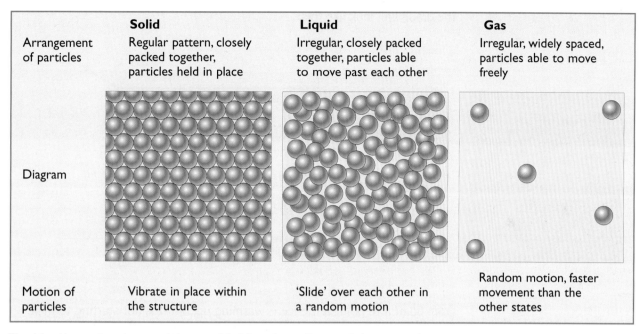

	Solid	Liquid	Gas
Arrangement of particles	Regular pattern, closely packed together, particles held in place	Irregular, closely packed together, particles able to move past each other	Irregular, widely spaced, particles able to move freely
Diagram			
Motion of particles	Vibrate in place within the structure	'Slide' over each other in a random motion	Random motion, faster movement than the other states

The **kinetic molecular model** uses this idea that all materials are made up of atoms that behave rather like tiny balls. And with this idea we try to build up a simple explanation (a 'model') of as much as possible.

When the model is used to try to explain the behaviour of gases it is often called the **kinetic theory of gases**, which we explore in the next chapter.

Melting and boiling

If you take a beaker that contains pieces of extremely cold ice and warm it up with an electrical heater, you can measure the temperature of the ice (and then water) every few seconds, and plot a graph of the temperature of the ice and water as the contents of the beaker warm up.

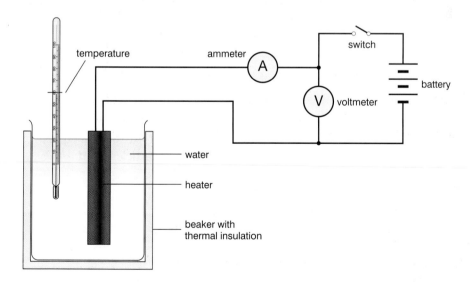

The graph will look like this:

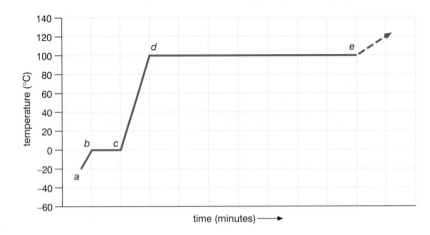

From point a to point b the ice is warming up, but it is not starting to melt. (This is similar to the behaviour of ice-cream after you take it out of the freezer, as it slowly takes heat out of the air and warms up without melting to begin with.)

Along line a–b, the heater is increasing the internal energy of the ice, and this is shown by the increase in temperature.

From point b to point c, the beaker contains a mixture of ice and water. The temperature stays constant, at 0 °C, and the heater melts the ice.

This makes a very important point. The energy from the heater has gone into the beaker, and so the internal energy of the contents of the beaker has gone up, but the temperature has not gone up. The energy has been used to melt the ice, and it is stored in the water. (In fact you have to put in almost as much energy to melt the ice as you will do, in the next step, to raise the water from freezing point to boiling point.) The same latent energy must be removed again to turn the water back into ice. (The word 'latent' means 'hidden'.) This is why it takes a freezer so long to freeze water.

From point c to point d, the input of heat energy into the water raises its temperature from 0 °C to 100 °C, and at point d the water boils.

In boiling, every particle in the liquid has enough energy to break away. This happens at a particular temperature – the **boiling point**. At the boiling point, the energy added to the material will be breaking the particles apart – the temperature does not change.

So from d to e the temperature of the boiling water stays constant, at 100 °C.

In this apparatus, the heater has to be turned off before all of the water is evaporated to prevent damage to the apparatus. But, in principle, if all of the steam could be retained, then after point e the heater could start to raise the temperature of the steam above 100 °C.

Condensation is the reverse of boiling, where the gas turns into a liquid, and solidification is the reverse of melting.

Note that it is coincidence that we live in surroundings that are at a temperature of around 20–30 °C. That is why we see that steam tends to condense to water, and ice tends to melt to water. If we lived on a really hot planet like Mercury, then all water would tend to turn to steam. And on a cold planet, it would all tend to turn to ice.

The extra energy stored by the water at 0 °C, as opposed to ice at 0 °C, is the **latent heat of fusion** of the water, and it is measured in joules. ('Fusion' is another word for melting.)

The heat required to melt a **unit mass** of solid and turn it into liquid is known as the **specific latent heat of fusion** of that solid, and is measured in J/kg or in J/g.

When you heat a liquid or a solid, and raise its temperature, the extra heat energy that you put in is stored as more vibration (in a solid) or more movement (in a liquid), as we have already discussed. Either way, it is definitely stored as a form of kinetic energy.

But while the solid is melting, the extra heat energy is used to weaken the bonds between the molecules and move the atoms slightly further apart against the attraction of the bonds. This energy is stored as potential energy, as in a stretched spring. So the internal energy of a liquid or a gas consists of some energy that is kinetic and some that is potential.

We use the term **latent heat of vaporisation** to describe the energy that is needed to change the state from liquid to gas at the boiling point of the liquid.

The latent heat of vaporisation is the additional potential energy carried by the gas, stored in the broken bonds between the molecules. Steam, not hot water, carries this extra energy. The extra energy makes steam very dangerous..

The heat required to turn a **unit mass** of liquid into gas is known as the **specific latent heat of vaporisation**, and is measured in J/kg or in J/g.

Evaporation

When particles break away from the surface of a liquid and form a vapour, the process is known as evaporation.

The more energetic molecules of the liquid escape from the surface. This reduces the average energy of the molecules remaining in the liquid and so the liquid cools down.

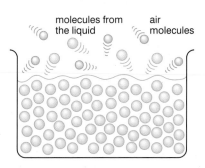

molecules from the liquid   air molecules

Evaporation causes cooling. The evaporation of sweat helps to keep a body cool in hot weather. The cooling obtained in a refrigerator is also due to evaporation of a special liquid inside the cooling panel at the back of the compartment. The vapour is collected, compressed back into liquid by a pump and recycled.

Clouds are formed from invisible water vapour that evaporates from the sea and is carried away by the wind. When the water vapour cools at high altitude, it turns back into the small droplets of water that you can see as these clouds.

Evaporation is increased at higher temperatures and it is also increased by a strong flow of air across the surface of the liquid, as in this way the evaporating molecules are carried away quickly. A certain amount of water will also evaporate more quickly if you increase its surface area. A bowl of soup will cool down much more quickly than a mug of soup, because the large surface area of the bowl allows more evaporation.

REVIEW QUESTIONS

Q1 Use ideas about particles to explain why:
  a solids keep their shape, but liquids and gases don't
  b solids and liquids have a fixed volume, but gases fill their container.

Q2 A student sets up an experiment. She places three shallow dishes each containing a small amount of water on the ground. Dish A is in the shade and out of any draught; dish B is in the light from the sun; and dish C is both in the light from the sun and it is exposed to a strong wind.
  a She measures the levels in the three dishes every hour. What will she observe?
  b Explain her observations using the molecular model.
  c She measures the temperature of dish B, and finds that it goes up after all of the water has disappeared. Explain why.

Q3 Using ideas about particles, explain the difference between evaporating and boiling.

More questions on the CD ROM

IDEAL GAS MOLECULES

In the **kinetic theory of gases**, we build up a set of ideas from the basic idea that a gas is made of many tiny particles, called **molecules**. These ideas give us a picture of what happens inside a gas.

Observed feature of a gas	Related ideas from the kinetic theory
Gases have a mass that can be measured.	The total mass of a gas is the sum of the masses of the individual molecules.
Gases have a temperature that can be measured.	The individual molecules are always moving. The faster they move (the more kinetic energy they have), the higher the temperature of the gas.
Gases have a pressure that can be measured	When the molecules hit the walls of the container they exert a force on it. It is this force, divided by the surface area of the container, that we observe when measuring pressure.
Gases have a volume that can be measured	Although the volume of each molecule is only tiny, they are always moving about and spread out throughout the container.
Temperature has an absolute zero.	As temperature falls, the speed of the molecules (and their kinetic energy) becomes less. At absolute zero the molecules would have stopped moving.

These ideas help to explain the three experimental gas laws.

Experimental gas law	Link to the kinetic theory
If the pressure of the gas stays constant, then the volume of the gas is proportional to its temperature. (Charles' law)	A higher temperature means the molecules move more quickly, so the force on the walls will be higher. If the pressure stays constant (pressure = force / area) and the force is higher, then the volume must increase to give a larger surface area.
If the volume of the gas stays constant, then the pressure of the gas is proportional to its temperature. (Pressure law)	A higher temperature means the molecules move more quickly, so the force on the walls will be higher. If the volume of the gas is constant (which means the surface area will stay constant), then the pressure (= force / area) must increase.
If the temperature of the gas stays constant, then the volume of the gas is **inversely** proportional to the pressure. (Boyle's law)	The temperature stays constant, so the average speed of the molecules stays constant. If the volume of the gas is reduced by half, then the molecules make the same number of collisions with half the surface area of wall, so the pressure (= force / area) must be doubled. This is **inverse** proportionality.

Gases *only* follow these rules if *three* conditions are met:

1 The mass of the gas must remain constant (i.e. no particles move in or out of the system).

2 The temperature must be measured using the **kelvin** scale.

3 Gases are ideal i.e. do not liquefy or solidify.

We will look at these ideas in more detail in the rest of this chapter.

Brownian motion

Evidence for the molecular model of matter comes from observations such as **Brownian motion**. In these experiments, small particles (such as pollen or fine smoke particles) can be seen moving in a random way. The explanation is that the particles are constantly being hit by even smaller particles, which are too small to see (such as water molecules or air molecules).

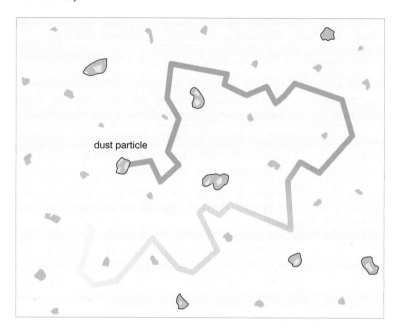

dust particle

Molecules in a gas

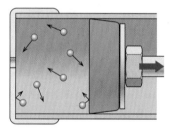

Let us see how these ideas can be used to explain the behaviour of gases.

The model says that the pressure on the walls of a container is caused by the collisions with the speeding molecules. You can feel this pressure if you try to hold a bicycle pump in the pushed-in position while blocking the air outlet with a finger. (If the pump is faulty and allows the air to escape, this does not work.)

In the diagram, the piston is *not* moving. However, there is a force trying to push it out. It is clear that if the molecules travel faster then they will hit the piston in the pump more often and harder. The pressure on the piston and on the walls will go up. This is exactly what will happen if the air gets hotter.

Note that, of course, the molecules will hit each other as well as the walls of the container. At normal pressures they travel a lot less than 1 mm between collisions. This does not affect the way that the model works.

The inner tube from a tyre has been pumped up with air before use as a toboggan. It is the pressure caused by the movement of the air molecules that keep it inflated. Because the temperature is low, the inner tube will have needed more air. On a hot day this tube could burst.

Absolute zero and the kelvin scale of temperature

As a material is cooled down, its molecules vibrate less, and (if the substance is a liquid or a gas) they move round more slowly. If you keep cooling the material down, it eventually reaches a temperature so low that even gases such as nitrogen and oxygen have turned into solids and all movement of the atoms in the solid has stopped. This temperature is the lowest that can be reached. It is known as **absolute zero**, and it has been shown to be at a temperature of –273 °C. There can be no lower temperature, as clearly the molecules cannot do less than not move!

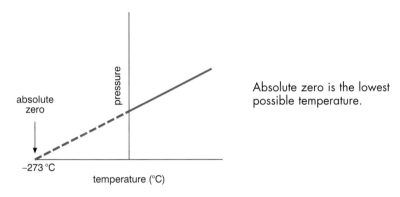

Absolute zero is the lowest possible temperature.

However, there are three subtle points that you may wish to note, although they do not change the above findings. First, scientists know that they will never cool anything quite as far as absolute zero, although they routinely reach just a millionth of a degree above it. Secondly, at absolute zero, the atoms will still be vibrating slightly with a last amount of movement that we can ignore because it absolutely cannot be removed from them. And, thirdly, helium, alone among the elements, will still be a liquid at absolute zero.

As there is an absolute zero, a system of measuring temperature has been set up in which the temperature at absolute zero is given the number 0. All other temperatures are then higher than this. As we make the steps the same size as in the celsius scale, you have to go up 273 degrees to reach the melting point of ice, and another 100 degrees to reach the boiling point of water. This scale is known as the **kelvin scale of temperature**.

The two temperature scales work like this:

Scale	Absolute zero	Melting point of ice	Boiling point of water	Melting point of gold
celsius	–273 °C	0 °C	100 °C	1064 °C
kelvin	0 K	273 K	373 K	1337 K

So to convert a temperature in degrees celsius to kelvin you add 273.

To convert a temperature in kelvin to degrees celsius, you subtract 273.

Note that the unit for the celsius scale is always called 'degree celsius' and written as °C, though you will sometimes see degC. The unit for the kelvin scale is **kelvin** and is always written as **K**.

The kelvin temperature scale may seem a strange invention, but it is very useful as it is closely aligned with the way that nature works. We will give two important examples of this.

Energy and temperature

We've already seen that the individual molecules of a gas are always moving. The higher the temperature of the gas, the faster they move (the more kinetic energy they have).

Although all of the molecules in a volume of gas are travelling at different speeds, it is possible to calculate the average speed of the molecules and hence their average kinetic energy. We know that the average kinetic energy of the molecules will increase as the temperature increases, but it is perhaps surprising to discover that the average kinetic energy is exactly proportional to the temperature of the gas in kelvin. So, for example, if the temperature of a gas is doubled from 273 K to 546 K, then the average kinetic energy of the molecules will exactly double as well.

Pressure and temperature

A second use for the kelvin scale is in calculating the effect on pressure in a sealed container. We know that the pressure in the container increases as the temperature goes up, but it is the kelvin scale again that describes exactly how. If you are using the kelvin scale, the pressure is proportional to the temperature. So if the temperature doubles, the pressure doubles. To put this into an equation:

$$p \propto kT$$

$$p = kT$$

where p stands for the pressure in the gas, T is the temperature in kelvin and k is a constant that depends on the size of the container and the amount of gas in it.

To solve a question, you need to know the equation:

$$\frac{p_1}{T_1} = \frac{p_2}{T_2}$$

where p_1 is the initial pressure and p_2 is the final pressure. These pressures must be in the same units, but they can both be in Pa or kPa or any other pressure unit. T_1 and T_2 (the initial and final temperatures) must be in kelvin.

WORKED EXAMPLE

A motor car tyre is filled to a pressure of 3 bar at 20 °C. After a long journey, the tyre reaches a temperature of 55 °C. What is the pressure now?

First we must convert the temperatures to kelvin. We could convert the pressures to pascal, but we choose to leave them in bar, where 1 bar is atmospheric pressure.

The initial temperature T_1 is (20 + 273) K = 293 K.

The final temperature T_2 is (55 + 273) K = 328 K.

The initial pressure p_1 is 3 bar.

Write down the equation: $\dfrac{p_1}{T_1} = \dfrac{p_2}{T_2}$

Substitute values into the equation: $\dfrac{3}{293} = \dfrac{p_2}{328}$

Rearrange the equation, and multiply both sides by 328 to find p_2:

$$\frac{p_2 \times 328}{328} = \frac{3 \times 328}{293}$$

$$p_2 = \frac{3 \times 328}{293}$$

Work out the answer and write down the units:

$$p_2 = 3.36 \text{ bar}$$

Note that the pressure does not go up very much, since (as measured in the kelvin scale) the temperature has not gone up very much. Tyre pressures should be measured with the tyre cold. They are designed to have this higher pressure when they are hot.

Pressure and volume

If the piston of a bicycle pump is pushed in with the air outlet blocked, then the more that you push it in, the harder and harder it gets to push it further. This is because the pressure in the container goes up.

piston moved in

The molecular model says there are the same number of molecules in the container travelling at the same speed. However, because the molecules are now packed in more densely, there will be more collisions with the walls and with the piston per second. If the volume is halved, then the number of collisions with the walls and with the piston will double, and the pressure on the piston will double. This law is often called Boyle's law. It only applies if the temperature of the air does not change.

A fixed amount of gas in a sealed container at constant temperature obeys the following equation:

pressure × volume = constant

pV = constant

p = pressure in Pa (or N/m^2)

V = volume in m^3

Pascals and newtons per square metre are the same thing. Apart from them, you can use whichever units you like so long as you stick with them.

The constant will be a constant for a particular sample of gas in a particular container. So, in an experiment (or an exam question) you can write that the initial values of pressure and volume multiplied together, $p_1 \times V$, are constant.

And the final values of pressure and volume multiplied together, $p_2 \times V_2$, are constant.

This is the same constant in both cases. Hence:

p_1V_1 = constant = p_2V_2

or

$p_1V_1 = p_2V_2$

This equation, Boyle's law, only applies if the temperature stays constant.

Now, as you may have noticed, air may heat up if it is compressed quickly. A bicycle pump can get very hot due to this effect. So the law strictly only applies if you let the gas cool down after compressing it, or you compress it very slowly. If you allow the gas to expand, it cools down, so you have to take precautions here as well.

WORKED EXAMPLE

A bicycle pump contains 400 cm³ of air at atmospheric pressure. If the air is compressed slowly, what is the pressure when the volume of the air is compressed to 125 cm³? What happens to the pressure if the air is compressed quickly? (Remember that atmospheric pressure = 100 kPa.)

Write down equation: $p_1V_1 = p_2V_2$

Substitute values into the equation: $100 \times 400 = p_2 \times 125$

$$p_2 \times 125 = 40\ 000$$

Rearrange the equation to find p_2: $p_2 = \dfrac{40\ 000}{125}$

Work out the answer and write down the unit: $p_2 = 320$ kPa

If the air is compressed quickly, it will also heat up to a higher temperature. This will mean that the final pressure will be greater than 320 kPa.

REVIEW QUESTIONS

Q1 How does kinetic theory explain the idea of absolute zero?

Q2 a Convert these temperatures from °C to kelvin.
   i 20 °C   ii 150 °C   iii 1000 °C
   b Convert these temperatures from kelvin to °C.
   i 300 K   ii 650 K   iii 1000 K

Q3 Cassie blows up a balloon. At room temperature, 20 °C, she measures the volume of the balloon as 1500 cm³. Then Cassie puts the balloon in a freezer where the temperature is −13 °C. Assuming the pressure stays constant, work out the new volume of the balloon.

More questions on the CD ROM

The Arctic Tern travels over 14,000 km in a year from the Arctic to the Antarctic and back again

Animal magnetism

How do migrating animals find their way? Arctic terns travel from the North Pole to the South Pole and back again each year; whales migrate from Hawaii to the northern Pacific coast and back. So why don't they get lost? A number of studies suggest that many animals have a magnetic sense that allows them to 'tune in' to the Earth's magnetic field.

The Earth behaves as if it has a giant bar magnet at its centre. Of course, there isn't really a rectangular block at the centre of the Earth, but the magnetic field does provide evidence that there is iron at the core. This magnetic core produces a magnetic field that extends through the surface and all around us. When we use a compass we are detecting these magnetic field lines. A material called biomagnetite has been discovered in the brains of a number of animals and it is thought that this allows the animals to sense the Earth's magnetic field and so find their way.

Animals use other techniques as well, such as sonar and sighting landmarks along the way, but it seems that some animals can use a compass, just like us. It's just that they carry their compass with them inside their bodies.

MAGNETISM AND ELECTROMAGNETISM

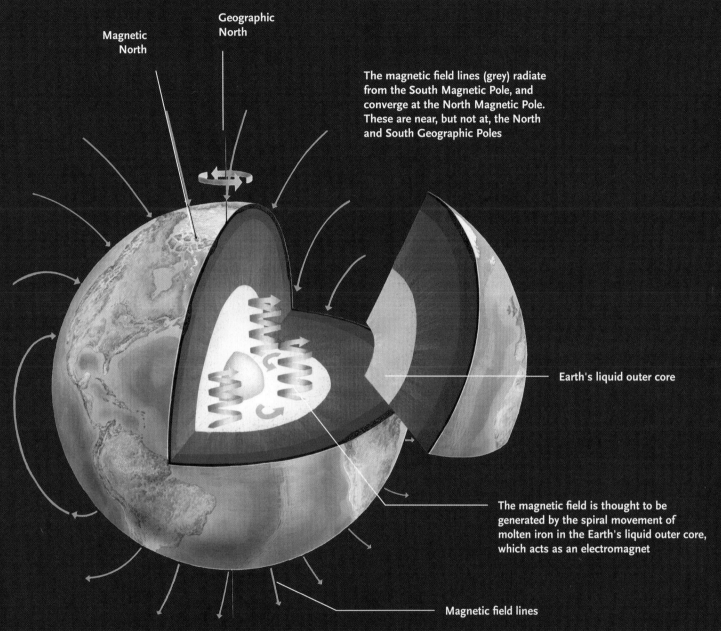

Magnetic North

Geographic North

The magnetic field lines (grey) radiate from the South Magnetic Pole, and converge at the North Magnetic Pole. These are near, but not at, the North and South Geographic Poles

Earth's liquid outer core

The magnetic field is thought to be generated by the spiral movement of molten iron in the Earth's liquid outer core, which acts as an electromagnet

Magnetic field lines

MAGNETISM

Videos & questions on the CD ROM

Magnets repel and attract

If a permanent magnet is suspended and allowed to swing, it will line up approximately north–south. Because of this, the two ends of a magnet (which are the most strongly magnetic parts) are called the north pole and the south pole, often labelled N and S. (Strictly, they are called the north-seeking pole and the south-seeking pole.)

If two north poles from different magnets are brought together, there will be a **repulsion** between them. The same happens if two south poles are used. However, if a north pole and a south pole are brought together, there will be an **attraction**. Magnets will also attract magnetic substances such as iron, nickel and cobalt.

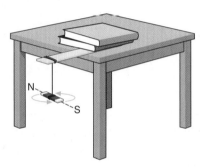

Magnetically hard and soft materials

There are several elements that are magnetic, the most important of which are iron, cobalt and nickel. Scientists have developed alloys and ceramics made from combinations of elements to get the exact properties that they want. Some of these materials are **magnetically hard** (such as steel, which is an alloy of iron and other elements such as carbon or tungsten). This means that they stay magnetic once they have been magnetised.

When we refer to a 'magnet', we mean **a permanent magnet** that is made of magnetically hard materials.

Other materials are **magnetically soft** (such as pure iron), which means that they do not stay magnetic – this is particularly useful in some electromagnetic devices such as the electromagnet and the relay.

Alloys are made by melting different metallic elements (iron, aluminium, copper, tungsten, etc) together. The resulting metal is known as a **ferrous** metal if it contains significant iron, and as a **non-ferrous** metal if it does not. Nickel and brass (copper + tin) are examples of non-ferrous metals.

In the past all magnetic materials were ferrous, but this is no longer true, and the strongest magnets may not contain any iron at all, for example, samarium-cobalt (SmCo), often used in headphones.

When we refer to 'magnetically hard' and 'magnetically soft' materials we are not referring to their physical hardness. You may have seen rubberised magnetic strips used on notice boards. These strips are permanent magnets, but are physically soft.

The headphones worn by this radio announcer will contain SmCo magnets.

Magnetic field lines

Magnets have a **magnetic field** around them – a region of space where their magnetism affects other objects. We describe the magnetic field using **magnetic field lines**. These lines show the path that a free north pole would take: heading away from a north pole and ending up at a south pole. The more concentrated the field lines are, the stronger the magnetic effect.

To show the field lines, place a bar magnet under a thin sheet of plastic, and sprinkle iron filings on to the top of the plastic. The iron filings will arrange themselves into strings of filings along the field lines.

It is also possible to follow the path of the field lines by placing a small compass (known as a plotting compass) on the plastic in place of the iron filings. If you move the compass in the direction that its north pole is pointing, then it will follow a field line.

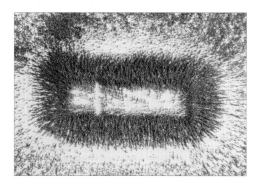

The iron filings show the field lines around a bar magnet.

Magnetic induction

If a soft magnetic material is brought near to a magnet it will be attracted. It has had magnetism **induced** in it; it has become **magnetised**. When the magnet is taken away, the material loses its magnetism again. Note that the magnet will continue to attract the soft magnetic material even if the material is turned round. This is the opposite behaviour to two magnets, as two magnets will repel each other in certain orientations. This simple method enables you to work out whether you are holding two magnets or one magnet and one piece of soft magnetic material.

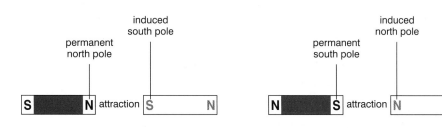

The pole of a permanent magnet always induces the opposite pole in an unmagnetised piece of magnetic material. So an induced magnet is always attracted to a permanent magnet.

Magnetic field patterns

The idea of field lines was first developed by the scientist Michael Faraday, the inventor of the electric motor. Note that where the magnets are repelling each other, the field lines do not go from one magnet to the other. Where the magnets are attracting each other, lines do cross from one to the other. This fact will help you to draw the lines more easily. It would be too much to say that the attraction is caused by the lines joining the magnets, but it almost seems like it.

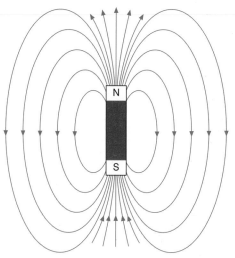

The magnetic field pattern of a bar magnet

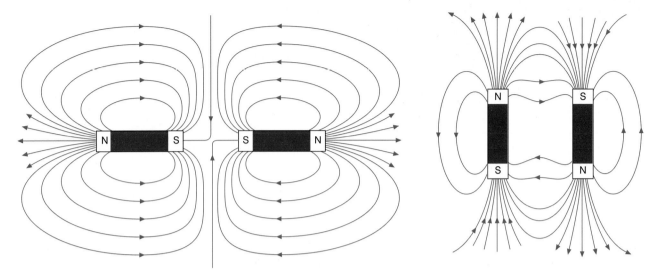

The magnetic field pattern
between two bar magnets

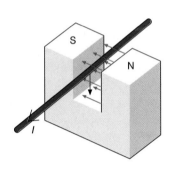

Uniform magnetic fields

If the two bar magnets are arranged with the N pole of one very close to
the S pole of the other, then many of the field lines will travel straight
from the one pole to the other. This will give a uniform magnetic field in
the gap between the two poles. You can get a similar field by using a
single bar magnet that has been bent round until its poles are close
together.

REVIEW QUESTIONS

Q1 What is the difference between a magnetically hard material and
a magnetically soft material? Give an example of each.

Q2 Ranjit has a piece of metal that he thinks is a magnet. He holds it
near another magnet and it is attracted. Ranjit says this proves
his metal is a magnet. Explain why Ranjit is wrong.

Q3 Sketch the magnetic field pattern for a single bar magnet. How
would the diagram change if the magnet were made stronger?

More questions
on the CD ROM

ELECTROMAGNETISM

Whenever an electric current flows along a wire, it produces a magnetic field around the wire. This fact makes possible the electromagnet, the loudspeaker, headphones, the electric motor, and many other inventions that are central to modern civilization.

Videos & questions on the CD ROM

Electromagnets

Electromagnets are made out of a coil of wire (often called a solenoid). When an electric current is passed through the coil, a magnet is formed with the N pole at one end of the coil and the S pole at the other end. If the coil is wrapped around a magnetically soft core, then when the coil is magnetised, it magnetises the core as well, and a very much stronger magnetic field is made. When the current is switched off, the coil loses its magnetism, so the core does as well.

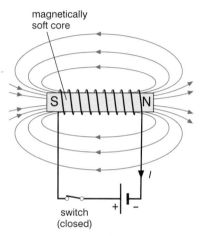
magnetically soft core

Electromagnet.

switch (closed)

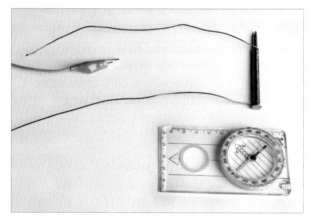

No current is flowing through the coil, and the compass points to the north.

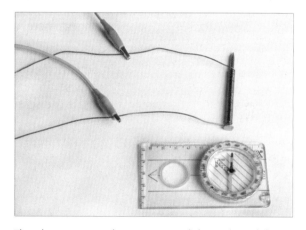

The electric current has magnetised the coil, and the coil has magnetised the soft iron core. The compass has lined itself up to the magnetic field.

Field patterns for electromagnets

If a wire is carrying electric current it generates a magnetic field around itself. The higher the current, the stronger the field. Some people believe that this field is a health hazard, particularly around high voltage distribution lines, but research into the topic has been unable to demonstrate any risk so far.

If the current is travelling along a long straight wire the field looks like this (below).

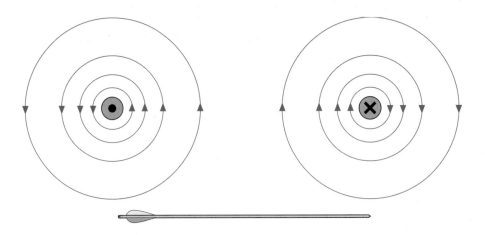

The dot in the centre of the wire indicates that the current is travelling directly towards you; the 'x' indicates that the current is travelling directly away. To remember this, think of an arrow. The dot is the tip of the arrow coming towards you, the 'x' is the flights on the tail of the arrow.

The field lines form continuous rings around the wire all along its length. The lines are shown closest together near to the wire, because the field is strongest there, and quickly gets smaller further away from the wire.

If the current is travelling towards you, the magnetic field lines are going in an anticlockwise direction, and if away from you they are going clockwise. To remember this, think of a woodscrew or a corkscrew. In both cases, if the screw is travelling away from you it is going clockwise.

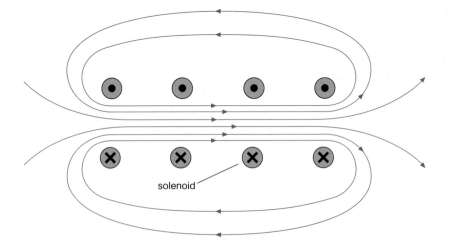

solenoid

We are using the **conventional current**, so remember that the electrons are *actually* going in the opposite direction.

We have already discussed the fact that an electric current flowing through a coil of wire (a **solenoid**) creates a magnetic field that looks very similar to the field from a bar magnet. If we were to cut a cross-section through a solenoid, it would look like the diagram (above). The current through the wires is marked as above.

With the current flowing as shown, the magnetic field lines are coming out of the right-hand end of the solenoid, and this is the north pole of the solenoid. To identify which end is the north pole and which end is the south pole, look directly at the end of the magnet and see which way the conventional current is circulating. There is an easy way to remember which is which: the direction arrows of the current can be incorporated into an 'N' or an 'S' (see below).

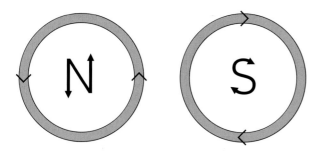

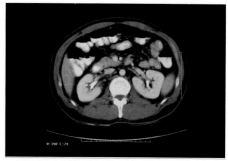

The magnetic field inside the solenoid is remarkably uniform, and this is used in the MRI scanner to allow doctors to produce images of the inside of the body. To do this the whole body has to be placed inside the solenoid.

To make the field stronger, you need more turns in the solenoid, and more current through the turns. (And adding a soft iron core makes a big difference as well.) If you reverse the current, the N and S poles will change ends.

It is also possible to make flat circular coils. These are like very short solenoids, with one face as a N pole and the other face as a S pole. The field lines thread through the aperture in the middle of the flat circular coil and then back around the outside – very much the same as a solenoid, in fact.

Force on a charged particle in a magnetic field

If a charged particle, usually an electron, is stationary in a magnetic field, it does not experience any force from the field. So if a copper wire that is full of electrons is placed near a magnet, nothing happens. However, if the charged particle starts to move through the field, then it will experience a sideways force that will try to push it off its path.

This is how a cathode ray tube (CRT) works in a TV and other equipment. Electrons are fired from the back towards a phosphor screen at the front that glows when hit by the electrons. The electrons form a spot on the screen, and this spot is steered by flat circular coils on the sides of the CRT so that it scans all over the back of the screen. It scans over the screen 50 or 60 times per second.

You can check this by putting a magnet anywhere near the CRT. The image will be horribly distorted as the electrons are pushed off their paths. (Make sure that you have the permission of the owner of the TV if you want to try this, as the image could be upset for several days, and could just possibly be permanently damaged.)

Force on a current-carrying wire

If a wire that is carrying an electric current is put in a magnetic field, then the moving electrons will be pushed sideways, and the whole wire will experience a sideways force. This effect is used to drive the loudspeaker, and to make the electric motor work.

A loudspeaker

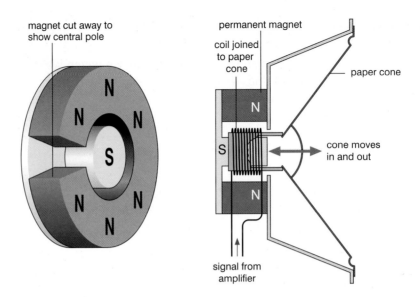

An **electric motor** transfers electrical energy to kinetic energy. It is made from a coil of wire positioned between the poles of two permanent magnets. When a current flows through the coil of wire, it creates a magnetic field, which interacts with the magnetic field produced by the two permanent magnets. The two fields exert a force that pushes the wire at right angles to the permanent magnetic field.

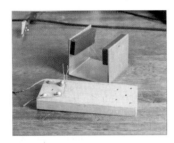

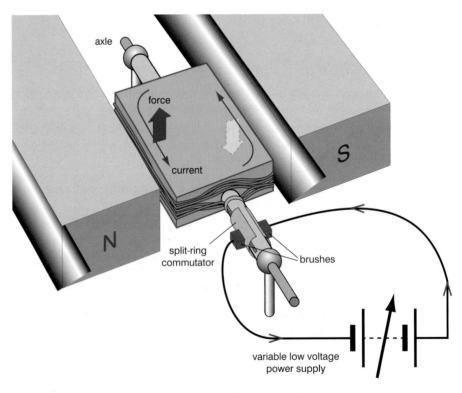

Making an electric motor

A motor coil as set up in the diagram will be forced round as indicated by the arrows (1 and 2 opposite). The split-ring commutator ensures that the motor continues to spin. Without the commutator, the coil would rotate 90° and then stop. This would not make a very useful motor. The commutator reverses the direction of the current at just the right point (3) so that the forces on the coil flip around and continue the rotating motion (4).

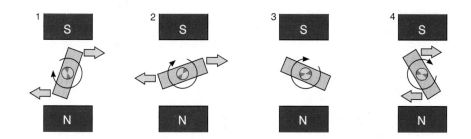

PREDICTING THE DIRECTION OF A FORCE

If a wire carrying an electric current passes through a magnetic field, with the field at right-angles to the wire, then the wire will experience a sideways force at right-angles both to the wire and to the magnetic field.

You should convince yourself that Fleming's left-hand rule gives you the correct answer for this diagram. Remember that the current is, as usual, the conventional current, and that the electrons are travelling the other way.

The size of the force depends on the magnitude of the current and the strength of the magnetic field. If you experiment with Fleming's left-hand rule you should be able to confirm that if you reverse either the magnetic field or the current then the force will be applied in the opposite direction, but that if you reverse *both* the field *and* the current then the force stays unchanged.

It is useful to look at the magnetic field lines for this set-up (below).

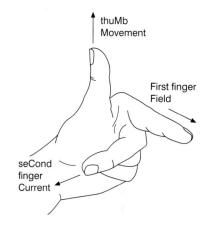

Fleming's left-hand rule predicts the direction of the force on a current-carrying wire.

The field lines from the magnet are pushed to one side by direction of the field lines from the wire. If you imagine that the lines are made of stretched elastic, then it is clear why the wire feels a sideways force.

If you check the diagram of the electric motor, you should be able to agree with the direction of rotation indicated.

FORCE INCREASES WITH FIELD AND CURRENT

The motor can be used to show how the force on the current-carrying wires varies if you change the conditions. If you increase the current or if you increase the strength of the magnetic field, then the force is larger and the motor spins faster. If you change the direction of the current or if you reverse the magnetic field, the direction of the force is reversed and the motor spins in the opposite direction.

REVIEW QUESTIONS

Q1 The diagram (below) shows a simple electromagnet made by a student.
Suggest two ways in which the electromagnet can be made to pick up more nails.

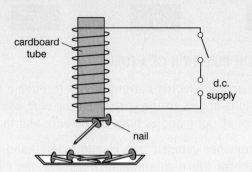

Q2 The diagram below shows an electric bell.
Explain how the bell works when the switch is closed.

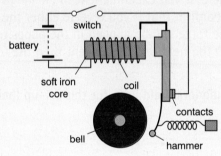

More questions on the CD ROM

ELECTROMAGNETIC INDUCTION

Michael Faraday was the first person to generate electricity from a magnetic field using **electromagnetic induction**. The large generators in power stations generate the electricity we need using this process.

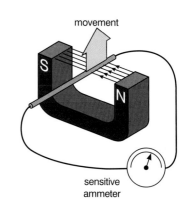

movement

S

N

sensitive ammeter

Current is created in a wire when:
* the wire is moved through a magnetic field ('cutting' the field lines), or
* the magnetic field is moved past the wire (again 'cutting' the field lines), or
* the magnetic field around the wire changes strength.

Current created in this way is said to be **induced**.

The faster these changes, the larger the current.

So the size of the current depends on the field strength and the speed with which the wire is moved.

Generation of electricity

In practice, the changes are induced in a coil of wire, because the current created is increased by the number of turns of wire in the coil. In this case the current is created by the change in the number of field lines going through the coil as the coil or the magnet rotates. The magnitude of the current generated is set by the rate at which field lines are cut, and so it will depend on:

* the area of the coil (the larger the coil, the more field lines will be cut)
* the number of turns in the coil (each extra turn effectively increases the number of lines cut; but you cannot use too many turns because if the wire is too thin it will overheat from the current carried)
* the strength of the magnetic field
* the speed of rotation.

DYNAMOS

A **dynamo** is a simple current generator. It looks very much like an electric motor. Turning the permanent magnet reverses the magnetism through the coil every time the magnet is rotated by 180 degrees. The changes in the magnetic flux through the coil induce an alternating current in the wires. The frequency of the electricity depends on the speed of the bicycle.

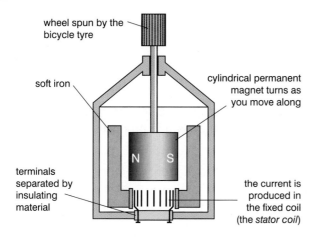

wheel spun by the bicycle tyre

soft iron

cylindrical permanent magnet turns as you move along

terminals separated by insulating material

N   S

the current is produced in the fixed coil (the *stator coil*)

In a bicycle dynamo, the magnet rotates and the coil is fixed.

GENERATORS

Power station generators do not have a commutator, so they produce **alternating current** (a.c.). Power stations use electromagnets rather than permanent magnets to create the magnetic field, and then pass the magnetic field through the rotating coils. The generator rotates at a fixed rate, producing a.c. at 50 hertz or 60 hertz, depending on the country.

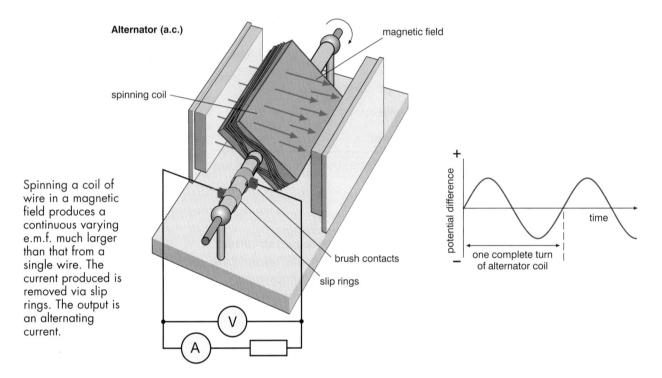

Alternator (a.c.)

magnetic field

spinning coil

brush contacts

slip rings

Spinning a coil of wire in a magnetic field produces a continuous varying e.m.f. much larger than that from a single wire. The current produced is removed via slip rings. The output is an alternating current.

potential difference

time

one complete turn of alternator coil

Transformers

A **transformer** consists of two coils of insulated wire wound on a piece of iron. If an alternating voltage is applied to the first (primary) coil, the alternating current produces a changing magnetic field in the core. This changing magnetic field induces an alternating current in the second (the secondary) coil.

If there are more turns on the secondary coil than on the primary coil, then the voltage in the secondary coil will be greater than the voltage in the primary coil. The exact relationship between turns and voltage is:

$$\frac{\text{primary coil voltage } (V_p)}{\text{secondary coil voltage } (V_s)} = \frac{\text{number of primary turns } (n_p)}{\text{number of secondary turns } (n_s)}$$

When the secondary coil has more turns than the primary coil, the voltage increases in the same proportion. This is a **step-up transformer**.

A transformer with fewer turns on the secondary coil than on the primary coil is a **step-down transformer**, which produces a smaller voltage in the secondary coil.

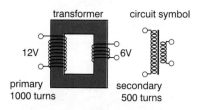

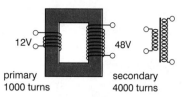

step-down transformer
ratio of number of turns is 2:1
voltage ratio is 2:1

step-up transformer
ratio of number of turns is 1:4
voltage ratio is 1:4

Transformers are widely used to change voltages.
They are frequently used in the home to step
down the mains voltage of 230 V to 6 V or 12 V.

WORKED EXAMPLE

Calculate the output voltage from a transformer when the input voltage is
230 V and the number of turns on the primary coil is 2000 and the number
of turns on the secondary coil is 100.

Write down the formula:	$\dfrac{V_p}{V_s} = \dfrac{n_p}{n_s}$
Substitute the known values:	$\dfrac{230}{V_s} = \dfrac{2000}{100} = 20$
Rewrite this so that V_s is the subject:	$V_s = \dfrac{230}{20}$
Work out the answer and write down the unit:	$V_s = 11.5\,V$

The current used by the transformer must change as well. No transformer
is 100 per cent efficient, because all transformers produce some heat when
they are working. But if it were 100 per cent efficient, then the electrical
power going in would equal the electrical power going out. That is to say:

primary coil voltage (V_p) × primary coil current (I_p)

= secondary coil voltage (V_s) × secondary coil current (I_s)

For example, if the output is 12 V, 10 A, that is 120 watts of power going
out of the transformer. If you know that the input voltage is 240 V, then
the input current will be 0.5 A.

Transmitting electricity

Most power stations **burn fuel** to heat water into high-pressure steam,
which is then used to drive a **turbine**. The turbine turns an a.c. generator,
which produces the electricity.

This turbine will be turned by water taken from a reservoir behind a dam. The a.c. generator will be fitted to the top of a turbine.

To minimise the power loss in transmitting electricity, the current has to be kept as low as possible. The higher the current, the more the transmission wires will be heated by the current and the more energy is wasted as heat.

This is where transformers are useful. This is also the reason that mains electricity is generated as alternating current. When a transformer steps up a voltage, it also steps down the current and vice versa. Power stations generate electricity with a voltage of 25 000 V. Before this is transmitted, it is converted by a step-up transformer to 400 000 V. This is then reduced by a series of step-down transformers to 230 V before it is supplied to homes.

Mains electricity is a.c. so that it can be easily stepped up and down. High-voltage/low-current transmission lines waste less energy than low-voltage/high-current lines.

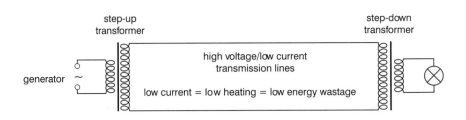

ENERGY LOSSES IN CABLES

With the exception of some lengths of superconducting cable (which has zero resistance but needs to be kept at a temperature below –200 °C) the distribution cables used by the electricity companies do not have zero resistance. A typical cable with a length of 100 km may have a resistance of 4 ohms. Now consider the problem facing the company when they want to send 4 MW of power to a town 100 km away. They must send either 10 A at 400 000 V, or 160 A at 25 000 V, or 17 400 A at 230 V.

Well, the 230 V solution is completely hopeless. To send 17 400 A through a resistor of 4 ohms requires a p.d. across the wire of 68 000 V. So almost all of the power from the power station would be used in the cables.

At 25 000 V, the p.d. across the cable would be:
$V = I \times R$
    $= 60 \times 4$
    $= 640$ V

The power lost in the cables would be:
$P = V \times I$
    $= 640 \times 160$
    $= 102\ 000$ W

Of the 4 000 000 W being sent, this is 2.6 per cent. This is not too bad, as electricity supply companies expect to lose a total of 5–10 per cent of the power that they generate between the power station and the customer.

At 400 000 V, 10 A, the power lost in the cables is just 400 W, which is 0.01 per cent of the power being sent. These cables will cost more, and so the electricity company will have to work out which high voltage solution is best.

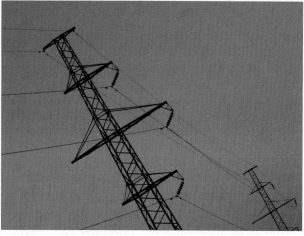

This 400 000 V distribution power line absorbs very little of the power that it carries, but it cost perhaps US$ 500 000 per km to build.

REVIEW QUESTIONS

Q1 The diagram (below) shows a transformer.
   a What material is used for the transformer core?
   b What happens in the core when the primary coil is switched on?
   c What happens in the secondary coil when the primary coil is switched on?
   d If the primary coil has 12 turns and the secondary coil has 7 turns, what will the primary voltage be if the secondary voltage is 14 V?

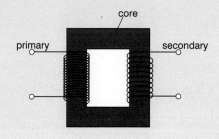

Q2 Two students are using the equipment shown in the diagram (below). They cannot decide whether it is an electric motor or a generator. Explain how you would know which it is.

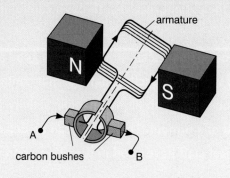

More questions on the CD ROM

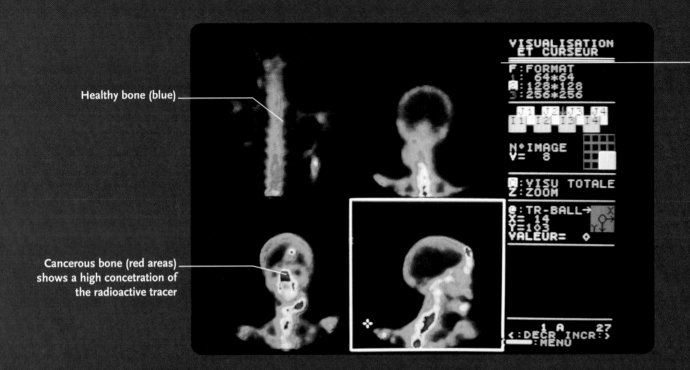

Healthy bone (blue)

Cancerous bone (red areas) shows a high concetration of the radioactive tracer

Seeing inside the body

Using radioactivity to 'see' inside people? Isn't radioactivity dangerous?

Strange as it may sound, using radioactivity, particularly gamma radiation, provides a powerful tool to help medical staff during diagnosis. Whilst it is true that gamma radiation can have harmful effects on living tissue, gamma imaging can provide information about what is happening inside a patient without the need for surgery. This non-invasive method is therefore quicker and overall has less risks than surgery. Of course, care is taken to minimise the radiation the patient receives, through careful monitoring of the dose and using a material with a suitable half-life

So how does it work? For an example, think about a bone scan. Bone tissue is good at absorbing phosphorus compounds, so the patient is injected with a radioactive material that contains phosphorus. This material will collect and form 'hot spots' at bone sites with high metabolic activity. High metabolic activity in bones might be connected to the growth of a tumour. These sites can be detected from outside the body using a gamma detector and so the medical staff have good information upon which to base further investigations.

RADIOACTIVITY AND PARTICLES

Gamma camera scans of the skull and spine of a
person suffering from multiple bone cancer.
This colour-coded image represents the position and
intensity of radiation emitted from a short-lived
radioactive tracer that concentrates in bone – more
strongly so in cancerous bone

RADIOACTIVITY

Videos & questions on the CD ROM

The structure of an atom

All elements are made up of atoms, consisting of protons, neutrons and electrons. The protons and electrons have electrical charges that are exactly equal but opposite. Because atoms, in general, do not have an electric charge, they usually contain the same number of protons and electrons.

The nucleus is made of protons and neutrons, bound together by an extremely strong force, far stronger than gravity, magnetism or electricity, and completely different from any of them. The electrons form a loose cloud on the outside of the atom with the nucleus in the middle.

To summarise:

Particle:	Proton	Neutron	Electron
Relative mass:	1.0	1.001	$\frac{1}{1838}$
Charge:	+1	0	−1

Atomic number, mass number and isotopes

The behaviour of the atom is fixed by the nucleus. Each nucleus is represented by its chemical symbol with two extra numbers written before it. Here is the symbol for Radium-226:

the top number is the **mass number** (the total number of protons and neutrons)

$$^{226}_{88}Ra$$

the bottom number is the **atomic number** (the number of protons)

It is common for several different nuclides (different nuclei) to have the same number of protons but different numbers of neutrons. For example, there are two types of copper nuclei, $^{63}_{29}Cu$ and $^{65}_{29}Cu$. The first type contain 29 protons and 63 nucleons (particles in a nucleus, i.e. protons and neutrons), hence (63 – 29) = 34 neutrons. The second type is the same except it contains 36 neutrons.

In naturally occuring copper, just under 70 per cent of the nuclei are $^{63}_{29}Cu$, and just over 30 per cent are $^{65}_{29}Cu$. These are the two stable isotopes of copper. Because they both contain 29 protons, they are surrounded by 29 electrons in the same pattern. It is the structure of the electrons around the nucleus that fix how the chemistry will work, so these two isotopes have the same chemistry, forming blue crystals of copper II sulfate etc.

This copper statue contains 69 per cent $^{63}_{29}Cu$ nuclei and 31 per cent $^{65}_{29}Cu$ nuclei.

In addition there are various radioactive isotopes of copper. These have different numbers of neutrons so their nuclei are unstable. There are nine radioactive isotopes, with mass numbers that vary from $^{59}_{29}Cu$ to $^{69}_{29}Cu$. These two extremes are very unstable with half-lives of a few minutes. $^{64}_{29}Cu$ has a half-life of 12 hours. So all of the radioactive isotopes of copper are extremely radioactive. Some radioactive isotopes of other elements are much less radioactive, and have half-lives measured in years, if not thousands of years.

Types of radioactive decay

Inside the atom the central nucleus of positively charged protons and neutral neutrons is surrounded by shells, or orbits, of electrons. Most nuclei are very stable, but some 'decay' and break apart into more stable nuclei. This breaking apart is called radioactive decay. Atoms whose nuclei do this are radioactive.

When a radioactive nucleus decays it may emit one or more of the following:
- alpha (α) particles
- beta (β) particles
- gamma (γ) rays.

A stream of these rays is referred to as **ionising radiation** (often called nuclear radiation, or just 'radiation' for short).

Radiation measurement device with beta emitter, aluminium sheet and meter.

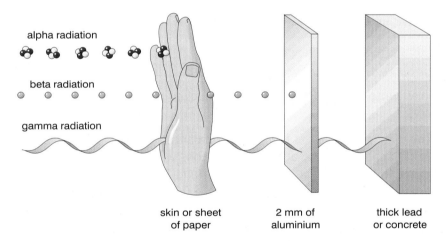

alpha radiation

beta radiation

gamma radiation

skin or sheet of paper   2 mm of aluminium   thick lead or concrete

	alpha (α)	**beta (β)**	**gamma (γ)**
Description	A positively charged particle, identical to a helium nucleus (two protons and two neutrons)	A negatively charged particle, identical to an electron	Electromagnetic radiation. Uncharged
Penetration	4–10 cm of air. Stopped by a sheet of paper	About 1 m of air. Stopped by a few mm of aluminium	Almost no limit in air. Stopped by several cm of lead or several metres of concrete
Effect of electric and magnetic fields	Deflected*	Deflected* considerably	Unaffected – not deflected*

* Note: Alpha particles and beta particles are deflected by magnetic and electric fields in the same manner that electrons are deflected in the cathode ray tube. These particles are travelling much faster so the deflections are smaller. Beta particles actually are electrons, so they are bent the same way. Alpha particles carry a positive charge, so they are bent the opposite way.

The effects of radioactive decay on a nucleus

An alpha particle contains two protons and two neutrons. So, with four nucleons and two protons, it is written as $^4_2\alpha$. It is the same particle as the nucleus of a helium atom, which is written ^4_2He.

When a nucleus emits an alpha particle it loses four nucleons, and its mass number decreases by 4. It loses two protons and its atomic number decreases by 2.

A beta particle is written $^{\ 0}_{-1}\beta$ to show that it has negligible mass and is of exactly the opposite charge to a proton. A beta particle is the same as an electron, and could be written $^{\ 0}_{-1}\text{e}$

When a nucleus emits a beta particle, a neutron inside the nucleus has changed into a proton plus an electron. The total charge is unchanged, but the nucleus has lost a neutron and gained a proton. The electron, of course, is emitted as the beta particle.

When a nucleus emits a gamma ray, it is a wave that is emitted as the nucleus reorganises itself inside. No particles are emitted, and so the mass number and the atomic number do not change.

Nucleus emits:	alpha particle	beta particle	gamma ray
Its mass number:	decreases by 4	does not change	does not change
Its atomic number:	decreases by 2	increases by 1	does not change

Nuclear equations

You can write down nuclear changes as nuclear equations. The rules are as follows:

- The numbers in the top row must be balanced on each side of the equation, because the number of nucleons will not change. (For example, you could get 231 on the left and 227 + 4 for an alpha emission, and 231 on the left and 231 + 0 on the right for beta emission.)

- The numbers in the lower row must be balanced on each side of the equation, because the total electrical charge will stay unchanged.

Here are two examples:

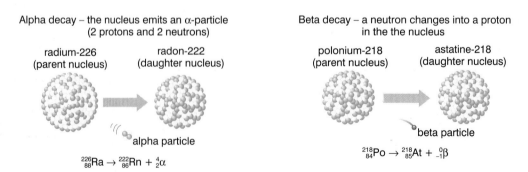

Alpha decay – the nucleus emits an α-particle (2 protons and 2 neutrons)

radium-226 (parent nucleus) radon-222 (daughter nucleus)

alpha particle

$$^{226}_{88}\text{Ra} \rightarrow {}^{222}_{86}\text{Rn} + {}^4_2\alpha$$

Beta decay – a neutron changes into a proton in the the nucleus

polonium-218 (parent nucleus) astatine-218 (daughter nucleus)

beta particle

$$^{218}_{84}\text{Po} \rightarrow {}^{218}_{85}\text{At} + {}^{\ 0}_{-1}\beta$$

Note particularly what happens when a beta particle is emitted. Because a neutron has changed into a proton, the atomic number has increased by 1!

Detection of radioactivity

All ionising radiation is invisible to the naked eye, but it affects photographic plates. Individual particles of ionising radiation can be detected using a Geiger–Müller tube.

There is *always* ionising radiation present. This is called **background radiation**. Background radiation is caused by radioactivity in soil, rocks and materials like concrete, radioactive gases in the atmosphere and cosmic rays, which come from somewhere in outer space, though we are still not sure *exactly* where.

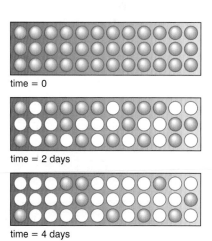

Radioactivity is measured using a Geiger–Müller tube linked to a counter.

Decreasing activity over time

The **activity** of a radioactive source is the number of ionising particles it emits each second. Over time, fewer nuclei are left in the source to decay, so the activity drops. The time taken for half the radioactive atoms to decay is called the **half-life**. Note that this time is the same whenever you choose to start measuring the source of radioactivity.

The level of radioactivity is measured in **becquerel**. A source that is one becquerel (written as 1 Bq) has one nucleus decay and emit radiation per second. A source in a laboratory may be a few hundred Bq, but industrial sources can be several kBq, if not MBq or GBq.

Half-life

Starting with a pure sample of radioactive atoms, after one half-life half the atoms will have decayed. The remaining undecayed atoms still have the same chance of decaying as before, so after a second half-life half of the remaining atoms will have decayed. After two half-lives a quarter of the atoms will remain undecayed.

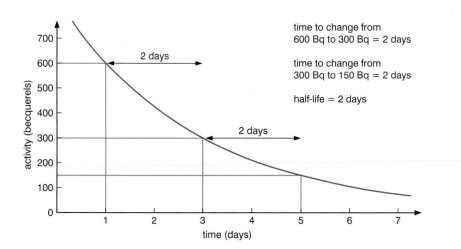

time to change from
600 Bq to 300 Bq = 2 days

time to change from
300 Bq to 150 Bq = 2 days

half-life = 2 days

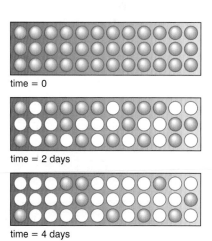

The half-life is 2 days. Half the number of radioactive atoms decays in 2 days.

WORKED EXAMPLE

A radioactive element is detected by a Geiger–Müller tube and counter as having an activity of 400 counts per minute. Three hours later the count is 50 counts per minute. What is the half-life of the radioactive element?

Write down the activity and progressively halve it. Each halving of the activity is one half-life:

0	400 counts
1 half-life	200 counts
2 half-lives	100 counts
3 half-lives	50 counts

3 hours therefore corresponds to 3 half-lives and 1 hour therefore corresponds to 1 half-life.

Uses of radioactivity

Gamma rays can be used to kill bacteria. This is used in **sterilising** medical equipment and in preserving food. The food can be treated after it has been packaged.

A **smoke alarm** includes a small radioactive source that emits alpha radiation. The radiation produces ions in the air which conduct a small electric current. If a smoke particle absorbs the alpha particles, it reduces the number of ions in the air, and the current drops. This sets off the alarm.

Beta particles are used to monitor the **thickness** of paper or metal. The number of beta particles passing through the material is related to the thickness of the material.

A gamma source is placed on one side of a **weld** and a photographic plate on the other side. Weaknesses in the weld will show up on the photographic plate.

In **radiotherapy** high doses of radiation are fired at cancer cells to kill them. Here, as in the case of X-rays, the radiation that can cause cancer is also an important tool in treating it.

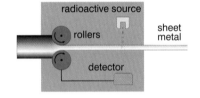

Sheet thickness control.

Tracers are radioactive substances with half-lives and radiation types that suit the job they are used for. The half-life must be long enough for the tracer to spread out and to be detected after use but not so long that it stays in the system and causes damage.
- **Medical tracers** are used to detect blockages in vital organs. A gamma camera is used to monitor the passage of the tracer through the body.
- **Agricultural tracers** monitor the flow of nutrients through a plant.
- **Industrial tracers** can measure the flow of liquid and gases through pipes to identify leakages.

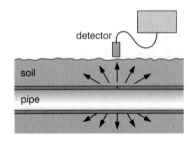

Tracers detect leaks.

RADIOACTIVE DATING

Igneous rock contains small quantities of uranium-238 – a type of uranium that decays with a half-life of 4500 million years, eventually forming lead. The ratio of lead to uranium in a rock sample can be used to calculate the age of the rock. For example, a piece of rock with equal numbers of uranium and lead atoms in it must be 4500 million years old – but this would be unlikely as the Earth itself is 4500 million years old.

Carbon in living material contains a constant, small amount of the radioactive isotope **carbon-14**, which has a half-life of 5700 years. When the living material dies the carbon-14 atoms slowly decay. The ratio of carbon-14 atoms to the non-radioactive carbon-12 atoms can be used to calculate the age of the plant or animal material. This method is called **radioactive carbon dating**.

USES OF ISOTOPES

Radioisotopes have the same chemistry as non-radioactive isotopes of the same element. This can be very valuable in research as well as medicine. A famous example is the use of radioactive iodine in treatment of cancer of the thyroid. The thyroid gland can become cancerous and the cancer then spreads through the body. Because the cells of the thyroid absorb far more iodine than other parts of the body, the cancer can be targeted by injecting the body with radioactive iodine. The iodine is absorbed by the cancerous cells wherever they are in the body, after which it kills them.

This woman's body was preserved in a bog in Denmark. Radioactive carbon-14 dating showed that she had been there for over 2000 years.

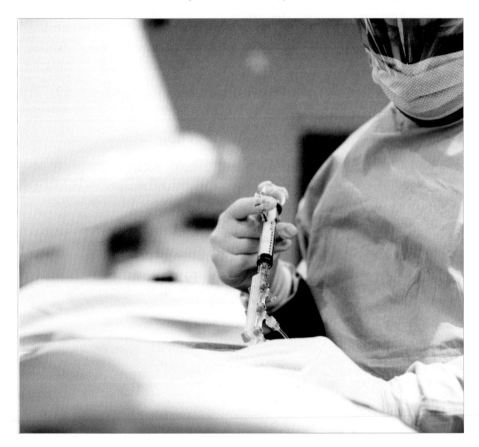

Radioactive iodine is injected in the treatment of cancer.

Dangers of ionising radiation

Alpha, beta and gamma radiation can all damage living cells. Alpha particles, due to their strong ability to ionise other particles, are particularly dangerous to human tissue. Gamma radiation is dangerous because of its high penetrating power. However, the cell has repair mechanisms that make ordinary levels of radiation relatively harmless.

Nevertheless, radiation can be very useful – it just needs to be used *safely*.

Safety precautions for handling radioactive materials include:
• Use forceps to hold radioactive sources – don't hold them directly.
• Do not point radioactive sources at living tissue.

- Store radioactive materials in lead-lined containers – and lock the containers away securely.
- Check the surrounding area for radiation levels above normal background levels.

High levels of radiation are extremely hazardous, and people handling highly radioactive materials must wear special film badges (containing photographic film) that monitor the dose that they are receiving. They may need to wear protective clothing, perhaps containing sheets of lead, and they will need to shower and check for radioactivity on their bodies at the end of each shift.

REVIEW QUESTIONS

Q1 Copy and complete this table to show the particles in these atoms.

Atom	Symbol	Number of protons	Number of neutrons	Number of electrons
Hydrogen	^1_1H			
Carbon	$^{12}_6C$			
Calcium	$^{40}_{20}Ca$			
Uranium	$^{238}_{92}U$			

Q2 The graph shows how the activity of a sample of sodium-24 changes with time. Activity is measured in becquerels (Bq).
  a Sodium-24 has an atomic number of 11 and a mass number of 24. What is the composition of the nucleus of a sodium-24 atom?
  b Use the graph to work out the half-life of the sodium-24.

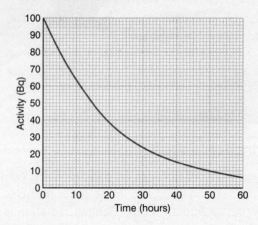

Q3 The following equation shows what happens when a nucleus of sodium-24 decays.

$$^{24}_{11}Na \rightarrow ^x_yMg + ^0_{-1}\beta$$

  a What type of nuclear radiation is produced?
  b What are the numerical values of x and y?

PARTICLES

Geiger and Marsden's experiment

At the beginning of the 20th century, scientists knew that the atom contained positive and negative charges, but the structure was a great mystery. An experiment by Rutherford discovered Rutherford scattering, and this cast great light on the structure.

(The actual work was done by two students of his, Geiger and Marsden. We were to hear more of Geiger later in his career.)

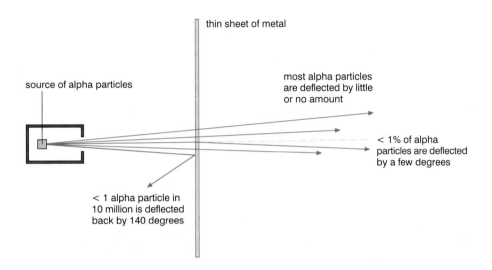

What they discovered was that almost all of the alpha particles got through the thin metal sheet with no difficulty, but that perhaps one particle in a million hit a relatively large object that sent it off at a wide angle, and perhaps even back the way it had come. This told them that the atom consists of a nucleus that contains almost all of the mass of the atom. Because so few alpha particles hit the nucleus, it had to be extremely small, surrounded by a cloud of extremely light electrons.

Rutherford's nuclear model

We are left with the slightly disturbing thought that almost all of a solid object is actually empty space, loosely filled with electrons, with a tiny nucleus at the centre of each atom. In a neutron star, where all of the atoms collapse, the whole star can end up perhaps 10 km across, with a density of 300 *million* tonnes per cubic centimetre.

The nucleus is made of protons and neutrons, bound together by an extremely strong force, far stronger than gravity, magnetism or electricity, and completely different from any of them.

Nuclear fission

A few nuclides have the strange property that they will split in two if they are hit by a neutron. This property is called **fission**. What makes it of great practical importance is that when the nuclide splits:

- it gives out a lot of energy in the form of a high kinetic energy (K.E.) of all of the parts that are created; this K.E. quickly turns into internal energy that can be extracted as heat.

- it gives out two or three more neutrons that will split more atoms.

One of just a few nuclides with this ability is the uranium isotope U–235. The equation for a typical reaction is:

$$^{235}_{92}U + ^{1}_{0}n = ^{137}_{56}Ba + ^{97}_{36}Kr + ^{1}_{0}n + ^{1}_{0}n + Q$$

You will notice that this equation is balanced by the rules that we gave above. Note, by the way, that the neutron has a mass of 1, and no charge.

So the starting point is uranium metal; after the split, we end up with barium metal and krypton gas. In this reaction, two neutrons are emitted, along with a lot of kinetic energy (represented by the letter Q).

The U–235 will split in one of many possible alternative ways. Instead of ending up as barium and krypton, it could turn into alternatives such as lanthanum and bromine, or cesium and rubidium. But generally both products will be radioactive, and two or three neutrons are emitted.

A chain reaction

If the neutrons emitted by a U–235 atom strike other atoms and cause them to split, then a chain reaction will occur. Consider the case where each atom causes two more atoms to split. When these two atoms split, they will cause four atoms to split, and then 8, 16, 32, 64, 128, etc. And more and more heat will be generated by the reaction. This uncontrolled chain reaction will cause an explosion, which is not what is wanted in a nuclear power station.

You can set up a row of dominoes so that each domino knocks down one further domino. This is a controlled chain reaction. You can also try setting up the dominoes so that one domino knocks down two dominoes, which then knock down four, etc. If you succeed you will get something more like an uncontrolled chain reaction.

Instead we want a chain reaction where every atom causes just one further atom to split. In this way you can get the steady heat that can generate electricity.

The nuclear reactor

Inside the reactor are the following components:

- **Fuel rods.**
  The uranium fuel is assembled into rods so that the rods can easily be inserted and removed to load and unload the reactor. Each rod is used for a few months until the U-235 is spent.

- **Control rods.**
  These rods are made of a metal that absorbs neutrons, such as cadmium or boron. If the rods are fully inserted, the chain reaction stops. If the rods are moved out, the reaction starts going faster and faster.

- **Moderator.**
  The gaps between the fuel rods and control rods are filled with a moderator such as carbon or heavy water. The job of the moderator is to slow down the neutrons emitted by the U-235, as otherwise they will be going too fast and will escape from the reactor without creating fission. It may seem strange that a neutron can be going *too fast* to split an atom of U-235, but this is so.

You will also need cooling to remove the heat. This is done by flowing pressurised water or another fluid through the reactor. In a power station, the exhaust from the reactor is used to boil further water for the turbines.

As a final note, it may seem to you that a nuclear power station is a dangerous device, only one step away from an explosion. This is not so. When you remove the control rods, the chain reaction only builds up slowly, over minutes or hours. Nothing can happen quickly. And reactors are equipped with many ways of shutting down within seconds. You may have heard of the disastrous explosion at Chernobyl in 1986. This is the biggest disaster in a nuclear reactor to date, but it took hours of unauthorised testing by incompetent operators before the reactor (already known to be an extremely unsatisfactory design) was taken to the point where it exploded. The environmental damage was severe, but as of 2004, there had been only 56 deaths as a result of the accident.

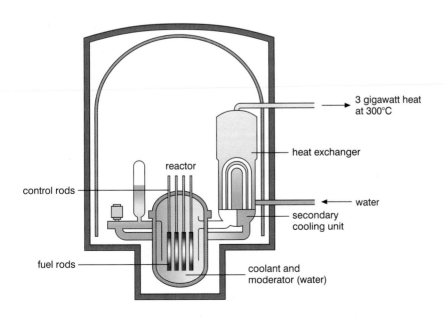

Nuclear power stations will continue to be a source of controversy, but the fact remains that they are extremely important. They generate 17 per cent of the world's electricity, and they have prevented the release of millions of tonnes of carbon dioxide and sulfur dioxide from coal and oil into the Earth's atmosphere.

Nuclear power can generate enormous quantities of energy from the radioactivity inside elements, uranium in particular.

QUESTIONS

Q1 What type of radiation is used in
a smoke detectors,
b thickness measurement,
c weld checking?

Q2 This question is about tracers.
a What is a tracer?
b The table right shows the half-life of some radioactive isotopes.

Radioactive isotope	Half-life
lawrencium-257	8 seconds
sodium-24	15 hours
sulphur-35	87 days
carbon-14	5700 years

Using the information in the table only, state which one of the isotopes is most suitable to be used as a tracer in medicine. Give a reason for your choice.

Q3 a When uranium-238 in a rock sample decays what element is eventually produced?

b Explain how the production of this new element enables the age of the rock sample to be determined.

Q4 The diagram shows some of the results of an experiment using some very thin gold foil that was carried out by the scientist Sir Ernest Rutherford.

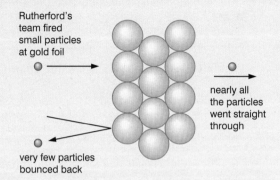

Rutherford's team fired small particles at gold foil

nearly all the particles went straight through

very few particles bounced back

a What type of radioactive particle did Rutherford use?

b What did Rutherford deduce from the observation that most of the particles passed straight through the foil?

c What did Rutherford deduce from the observation that some particles bounced back from the foil?

Q5 Scientists have a saying that 'most matter is empty space'. Explain what this means, using the ideas from Geiger and Marsden's experiment.

More questions on the CD ROM

EXAM PRACTICE AND ANSWERS

EXAM PRACTICE AND ANSWERS

EXAM TIPS

Read each question carefully; this includes looking in detail at any **diagrams, graphs** or **tables.**
- Remember that any information you are given is there to help you.
- Underline or circle the **key words** in the question and **make sure you answer the question that is being asked.**

Make sure that you understand the meaning of the **'command words'** in the questions. For example:
- **'Describe'** is used when you have to give the main feature(s) of, for example, a process or structure.
- **'Explain'** is used when you have to give reasons, e.g. for some experimental results.
- **'Suggest'** is used when there may be more than one possible answer, or when you will not have learnt the answer but have to use the knowledge you do have to come up with a sensible one.
- **'Calculate'** means that you have to work out an answer in figures.

Look at **the number of marks** allocated to each question and also the **space provided.**
- Include at least as many points in your answer as there are marks. If you do need more space to answer, then use the nearest available space, e.g. at the bottom of the page, making sure you write down which question you are answering. **Beware of continually writing too much because it probably means you are not really answering the questions.**

Don't spend so long on some questions that you don't have time to finish the paper.
- You should spend approximately **one minute per mark.** If you are really stuck on a question, leave it, finish the rest of the paper and come back to it at the end.

In short-answer questions, or multiple-choice type questions, **don't write more than you are asked for.**
- In some exams, examiners apply the rule that they only mark the first part of the answer written if there is too much. This means that the later part of the answer will not be looked at.
- In other exams you would not gain any marks if you have written something incorrect in the later part of your answer, even if the first part of your answer is correct. This just shows that you have not really understood the question or are guessing.

In calculations always show your working.
- Even if your final answer is incorrect you may still gain some marks if part of your attempt is correct. If you just write down the final answer and it is incorrect, you will get no marks at all.
- Also in calculations write your answer to as many **significant figures** as are used in the question.
- You may also lose marks if you do not use the correct **units**.

Aim to use **good English** and **scientific language** to make your answer as clear as possible.
- In short answer questions, just one or two words may be enough, but in longer answers take particular care with capital letters, commas and full stops.
- If it helps you to answer clearly, do not be afraid to also use **diagrams** in your answers.

When you have finished your exam, **check through** to make sure you have answered all the questions.
- Cover your answers and read through the questions again and check your answers are as good as you can make them.

EXAM QUESTIONS AND STUDENT'S ANSWERS (FOUNDATION TIER)

1 (a) Circle the names of two materials which are attracted to magnets.

aluminium   (brass) ✗   copper   (iron) ✓   steel   tungsten   [2]

(b) The diagram shows a pattern of lines around a magnet.

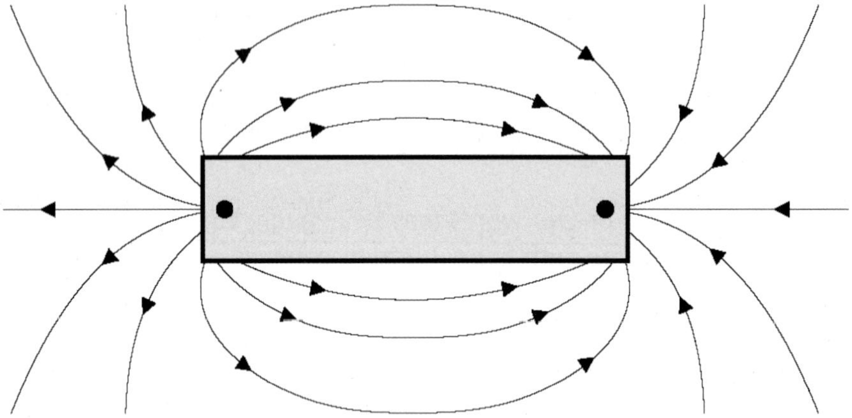

Name:

(i) this shape of magnet   *bar magnet* ✓   [1]

(ii) the points marked •   *north and south poles* ✓   [1]

(iii) the lines   *force lines* ✗   [1]

(c) Two magnets, like the magnet shown above, were used to get the pattern of lines shown below.

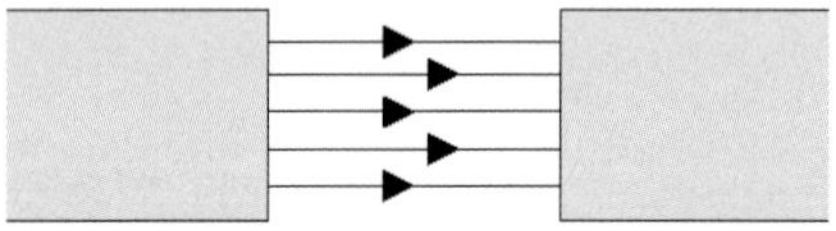

Describe what you would do with the two magnets so that you got this pattern.

Put them end to end so that the north faces the south. ✓ ✗   [2]

HOW TO SCORE FULL MARKS

a) One mark has been given for correctly choosing iron as a material that is attracted to magnets. Brass is incorrect – steel should have been the other choice from the list. There are only four magnetic metals – make sure you learn them carefully. **Also, the question asked for two names – make sure you do not give more than this.**

b) Two marks awarded. In part i) bar magnet is clearly acceptable, 'rectangular magnet' would also have scored the mark. In part ii), the key word is 'poles', the region of the magnet where the magnetism is strongest. The north and south given in the answer are correct and could even have been labelled on the diagram. Take care – writing 'north and south' on its own would *not* have scored the mark – 'north and south' are *directions* and can only score the mark here when the word 'poles' is added. In general, **make sure that you learn technical terms carefully and that you use the full**

term – this is where lots of practice questions can be very helpful. In part iii) no mark is awarded. The best answer would be 'magnetic field lines'. If the student had written '*magnetic* force lines' he or she would just have scored the mark, but as it stands it is wrong – there are many situations that might show 'force lines' without being linked to magnetism.

c) One mark is awarded. The student has correctly realised that the poles must be different for the magnetic field lines to form this pattern. However, the student has not made a second point about the situation – **always take notice of how many marks are available.** Possibilities for the second mark include: the north pole must be on the left (remember that field lines point from north to south) or that the magnets must be held apart (remember that the opposite poles would attract each other).

A mark of 4 out of a possible 7 corresponds to a grade F on this question.

QUESTIONS TO TRY (FOUNDATION TIER)

I a) In the box are the names of five waves.

| infra red   microwaves   ultrasonic   ultraviolet   **X-rays** |

Which wave is used to:

i)   send information to a satellite? [1]

ii)   toast bread? [1]

ii)   clean a valuable ring? [1]

b)   The diagram shows four oscilloscope wave traces. The controls of the oscilloscope were the same for each wave trace.

A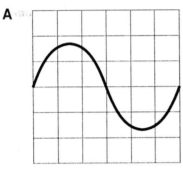

B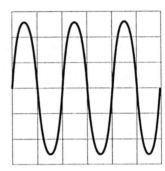

C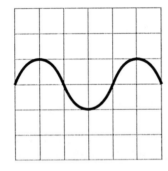

D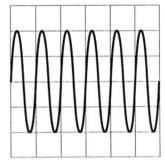

Which **one** of the wave traces, A, B, C or D, has:

i)   the largest amplitude? [1]

ii)   the lowest frequency? [1]

c) The diagram shows a longitudinal wave in a stretched spring.

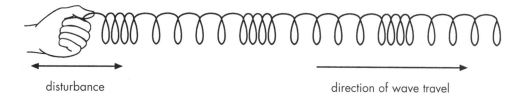

disturbance   direction of wave travel

Complete the sentence. You should put only **one** word in each space.

A longitudinal wave is one in which the .... causing the wave is

in the same .... as that in which the waves moves.   [2]

d) Which **one** of the following types of wave is longitudinal? Draw a ring around your answer.

light wave   **sound wave**   **water wave**   [1]

EXAM QUESTION AND STUDENT'S ANSWERS (FOUNDATION TIER/HIGHER TIER OVERLAP)

1 This question is about electrostatics.

a) There are two kinds electric charge.

Write down the names of both types of electric charge.

positive   and   negative ✔   [1]

b) Leon wants to charge his plastic comb.

Write down one way he could charge his plastic comb.

He could rub it.   ✔ ✗

[2]

c) Leon holds his charged comb near some small pieces of paper.

charged comb

paper

Suggest what might happen to the paper.

They stick to the comb.

[1]

d) Leon touches a metal radiator.

He gets an electric shock.

Describe how Leon gets an electric shock.

(One mark is for the correct use of scientific words.)

The metal radiator is electric and gives Leon a shock.   ✗ ✗ ✗

[2+1]

e) Leon paints cars.

Static electricity is useful in spraying paint.

i) Write down **one other** use of static electricity.

A photocopier ✔ _____   [1]

ii) Explain why static electricity is useful in spraying cars.

In your answer use ideas about electric charge.
(One mark is for linking ideas.)

The paint is charged when it comes out of the sprayer. The car is also
charged with the opposite charge. ✔ This makes the paint stick to the
car much better. ✔ _____   [3+1]

6/12

[Total 12 marks]

HOW TO SCORE FULL MARKS

a)   The correct response has been given. The symbols '+' and '−' would have been acceptable.

b)   'He could rub it' scores one mark, although 'by friction' would have been a stronger phrase to use. There is a second mark for saying that the comb should be rubbed against **an insulator** (or you could give an example of an insulator, such as cloth). **Always check the number of marks available.**

c)   One mark has been awarded for the correct response. The student indicates correctly that there will be an **attraction** between the comb and the pieces of paper.

d)   This is a very vague answer. There are three marks available. The student can score any two. The correct response needs to realise the **Leon** has become **charged** (perhaps by friction against a carpet), that these charges **move** when he touches the radiator, **from Leon to the radiator**. The third mark is for using correct scientific words. Relevant words here are: charging, electrons, earth, earthing.

e) i) One mark has been awarded. Alternative correct responses would include inkjet printers, dust precipitators or crop spraying.

ii) Two marks have been awarded. The student seems to have an idea of what is happening, but has failed to use the correct scientific terms accurately. One mark has been awarded for the idea that opposite charges attract, but saying the paint 'sticks' to the car is not accurate enough to gain a second mark – the student needed to say that the paint is **attracted** to the car. In a similar way, saying the paint covers 'much better' is too vague. At this level, the student should refer to the paint being attracted to **the whole object**, even parts not in a direct line, or that **less paint is wasted**. Another approach would be to state that **like charges repel** (one mark) and so the paint forms **a fine spray** (one mark), which produces **an even coat** (one mark).

- A mark of 6 out of a possible 12 corresponds to a grade D on this Foundation/Higher Tier Overlap question.

QUESTIONS TO TRY (FOUNDATION TIER/HIGHER TIER OVERLAP)

1

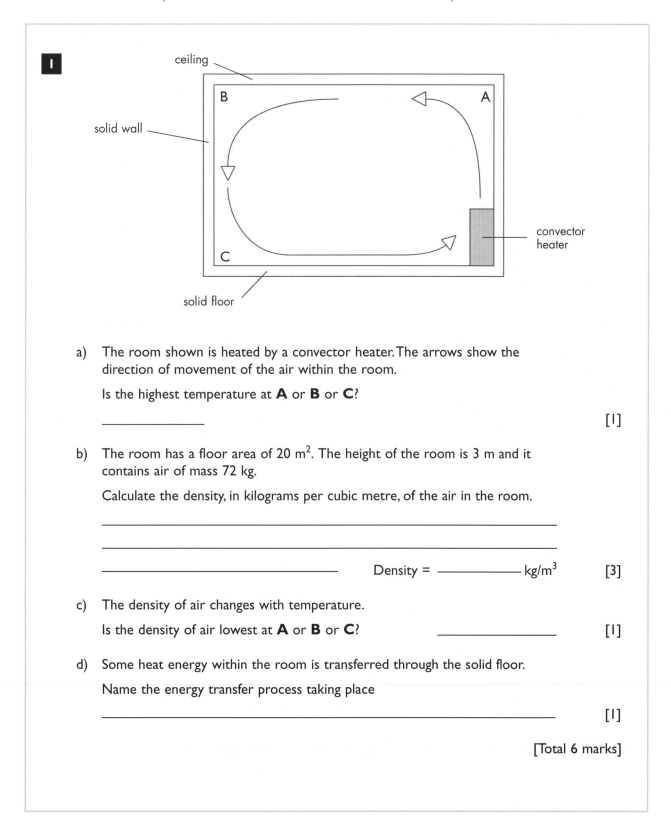

a) The room shown is heated by a convector heater. The arrows show the direction of movement of the air within the room.

Is the highest temperature at **A** or **B** or **C**?

_____ [1]

b) The room has a floor area of 20 m². The height of the room is 3 m and it contains air of mass 72 kg.

Calculate the density, in kilograms per cubic metre, of the air in the room.

_____

_____

_____ Density = _____ kg/m³   [3]

c) The density of air changes with temperature.

Is the density of air lowest at **A** or **B** or **C**?   _____ [1]

d) Some heat energy within the room is transferred through the solid floor.

Name the energy transfer process taking place

_____ [1]

[Total 6 marks]

EXAM QUESTIONS AND STUDENT'S ANSWERS (HIGHER TIER)

1 Fig. 1.1 shows a simple beam balance made from a pivot and a metre rule.

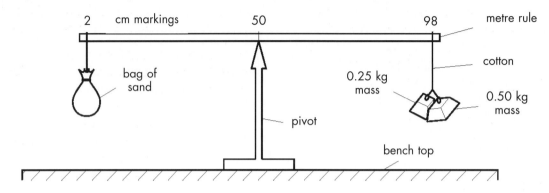

Fig. 1.1

a) Find

(i) the mass of the bag of sand,

mass = <u>0.75 kg</u> ✔

(ii) the weight of the bag of sand. (The acceleration of freefall is 10 m/s^2 .)

weight = <u>$m \times g = 0.75 \times 10 = 7.5$ N</u> ✔✔   [3]

(b) Explain, in terms of moments of forces, why the beam balances.

<u>because the masses are the same</u> ✔

✗ ✗

[3]

(c) The cotton holding the 0.50 kg mass snaps and the mass falls to the bench. It strikes the bench at a speed of 1.2 m/s.

Calculate its kinetic energy just before it hits the bench.

$\frac{1}{2} m v^2$

$= 0.5 \times 0.5 \times 1.2^2$

kinetic energy of the mass = <u>0.36</u> ✔✔✗   [3]

(d) On impact with the bench, the mass bounces up a small distance. Some transformation of energy occurs during the impact. State the forms of the energy just before and just after the impact.

before: <u>kinetic</u> ✔

after: <u>sound</u> ✔   [2]

[Total 11 marks]

HOW TO SCORE FULL MARKS

a) Three marks awarded. In part i) the student has realised that the sand and the masses are the same distance from the pivot. This makes the calculations much easier. For this part of the question, it means that the mass on the left-hand side of the pivot must be the same as on the right-hand side. Take care to include all the masses on the right-hand side! **Remember to write down the unit** (kg in this case) if there is a space for it. In part ii) the student has used the correct equation and has calculated correctly, so two marks given. The student has again given the correct unit.

b) One mark awarded – clearly this answer is too short. **Always check how many marks are available.** In this case three marks are available, so three points will be needed in the answer. **The number of lines given for the answer is usually a good guide to the length of response required.** The student does gain a mark (just) for saying the masses are the same – it would have been better to specify 'the masses hanging on either side of the pivot are the same'. The

student does not, however, go on to state that the masses are equal distances from the pivot (second mark) and so the turning effect, the moment, is the same on both sides (third mark).

c) Two marks awarded. The student uses the correct equation and calculates the value correctly. However, this time the student has not included the unit (joules, J), even though a space is provided, and so loses a mark. Remember that **almost all quantities in physics have a unit associated with them** – make sure you are familiar with them.

d) Two marks awarded. The question states that the mass has kinetic energy before the collision. After the collision, several possibilities exist. Some energy will be transferred as heat, the mass has bounced so it will still have some kinetic energy, it has bounced upwards so it has some gravitational potential energy. Since the question does not specify how many examples are required, it is probably best to keep the answer simple – **two marks are available, so give two answers.**

QUESTIONS TO TRY (HIGHER TIER)

1 Bobby goes on holiday in a caravan.

He uses a wind turbine to make electricity.

a) The turbine turns the simple a.c. generator shown below.

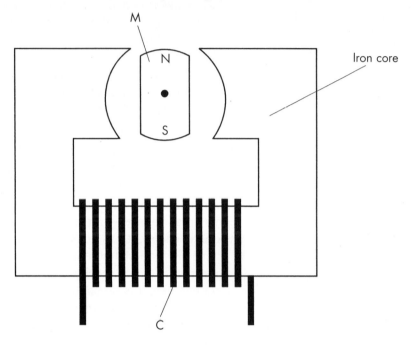

i)   The term a.c. stands for **alternating current**.
Explain the difference between alternating current and direct current.   [1]

ii) Explain how the simple generator shown above generates alternating current.
Include the names of the parts labelled **M** and **C**.   [4]

b) The generator is connected to the caravan by long cables.
Bobby is worried about energy losses in the cable.

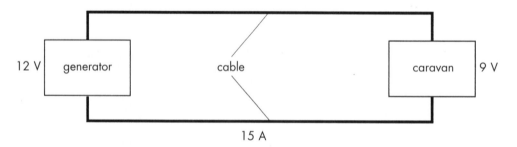

The generator produces a.c. at 12 V.

Bobby finds that when the current in the cable is 15 A, the voltage at the caravan is only 9 V.

i)   State the equation which links voltage, current and resistance.   [1]

ii) Calculate the resistance of the **cable**.   [2]

2 (a) All living things contain carbon atoms. All materials such as leather or wood, which come from living things, also contain carbon atoms. Of all these carbon atoms, a tiny proportion is carbon-14.

The nuclear equation for the radioactive decay of carbon-14 is

$$^{14}_{6}C \rightarrow \, ^{14}_{7}N + \, ^{0}_{-1}e$$

Beta particles are emitted in this decay. How can you tell this from the equation?

_____

_____

_____ [2]

(b) There are three forms of carbon: carbon-12, carbon-13 and carbon-14. Complete the sentence.

These three forms are _____ of carbon. [1]

(c) Radium-226 is a radioactive metal which decays by alpha emission to radon-222 which is a radioactive gas.

Complete the nuclear equation for this decay.

$$^{226}_{88}Ra \rightarrow \underline{\hspace{1cm}} Rn + \underline{\hspace{1cm}} He$$ [2]

[Total 5 marks]

3 A hot air balloon is tied to the ground by two ropes. The diagram shows the forces acting on the balloon.

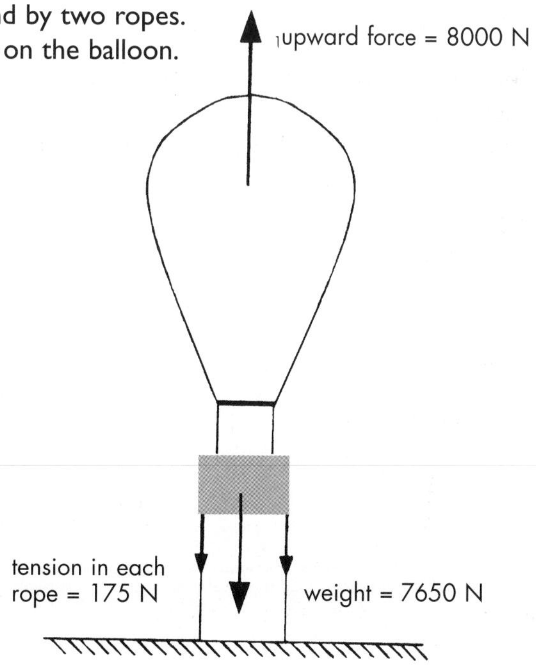

upward force = 8000 N

tension in each rope = 175 N

weight = 7650 N

The ropes are untied and the balloon starts to move upwards.

a) Calculate the size of the unbalanced force acting on the balloon. State the direction of this force. [2]

b) The mass of the balloon is 765 kg. Calculate the initial acceleration of the balloon. [3]

EXAM PAPER 3

This examination is designed to test your skills in **experimental physics**. A single exam covers both Foundation and Higher tiers.

You will need to **demonstrate** a number of experimental skills, including:

- How to read meters and other measuring devices
- How to plot graphs and interpret what they show
- How to perform straightforward experiments to organise the collection of sensible data

The experiments used in the exam paper may not be familiar to you, but you should be able to use ideas and experiences that you already have to answer the questions.

Be particularly careful that you use a sensible number of **significant figures** in your numerical answers. Your calculator will do the maths for you, but you need to apply your physics knowledge to give a meaningful answer. As a general rule, you should only be using two or three significant figures in your answers.

Don't confuse **significant figures** with **decimal places**.

EXAM QUESTIONS AND STUDENT'S ANSWERS (PAPER 3)

1 A student is asked to investigate the properties of three different cups.
The cups are all of the same size and shape but made from different materials.
These cups keep drinks hot for as long as possible.

She has the following apparatus.

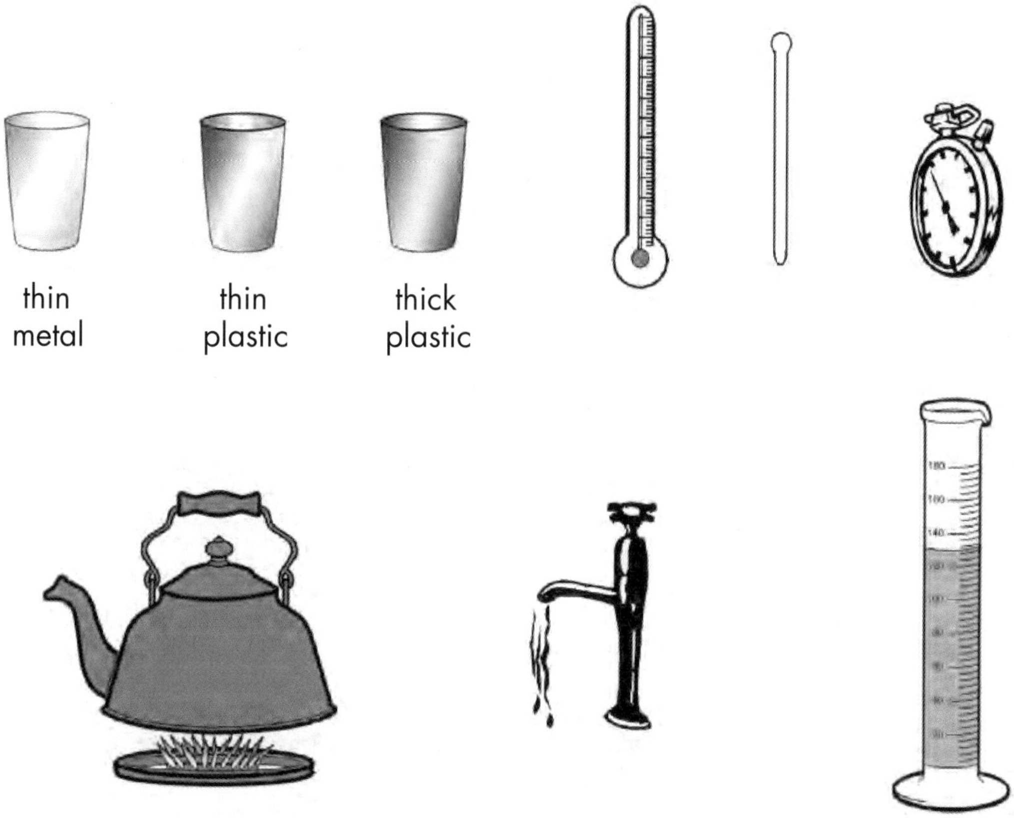

thin
metal

thin
plastic

thick
plastic

(a) Describe how the student would use the apparatus to determine which cup keeps the
liquid hottest. [8]

Put some water from the tap into the kettle ✔ and heat it up. ✔ Put some of the
hot water into one of the cups ✔. Measure the temperature of the water. ✔ Start
the stopwatch ✔ and wait for five minutes. Measure the temperature of the water
again. ✔ Repeat this process using both of the other cups. ✔

(b) List two things that she should keep constant when comparing cups in this investigation. [2]

1 the volume of water in the cup. ✔

2 the temperature of the water ✗

(c) During the investigation she takes readings from the measuring cylinder and the thermometer.
Record her readings. [2]

thermometer

68 °C

measuring cylinder

130 ml

(d) The student makes the following notes during the investigation with the three cups. [4]
List four criticisms of her recording of data and experimental method.

PLASTIC

32.46 °C after about half a minute

1   it doesn't say which kind of plastic ✓
2   the temperature should not be given to four significant figures ✓
3   the thermometer cannot measure this accurately ✗
4   the data would be better in a table ✓

EXAMINER'S COMMENTS

a) This is quite a thorough answer and scores 7 out of 8. The answer is arranged in a logical sequence, starting at the beginning of the experiment, heating the water, and then describing the steps in turn. The candidate would have scored full marks if they had, for example, stated that the temperatures should be measured **with a thermometer. Always try to think through the whole experiment before writing a sequence like this.** You could perhaps put you ideas roughly in bullet points to make the sequence more obvious.

(b) Mentioning 'in the cup' is important in the first answer to make it clear that you are not talking about the water in the kettle (which would not score a mark). In the second part, unfortunately, the candidate has made the mistake of being too vague – it is the temperature of the water **at the start** which needs to be kept constant.

(c) Two correct answers. **Always check the scales carefully** – some go up in ones, some in twos, some in fives, and so on.

(d) These are sensible comments. Unfortunately the second and third points are different ways of saying the same thing, so they only score one mark. Other points that would have scored a mark include a comment on the time being too vague or that the temperature given does not make clear whether it is a temperature change or the actual temperature after half a minute (in which case it would seem to be too low).

QUESTIONS TO TRY (PAPER 3)

1 The diagram shows part of a transformer. There are 10 turns of insulated wire wrapped around the right side of the core.

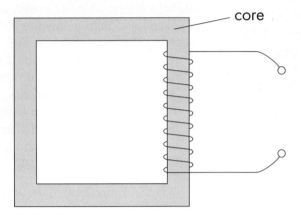

core

(a) Draw 5 turns of wire around the left side of the core. [1]

(b) Below are the symbols for an alternating current (a.c.) supply and a 0–10Va.c. voltmeter. Add these to the diagram to represent a step-up transformer from which the output voltage can be measured. [2]

 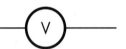

(c) When a student uses the apparatus as a step-up transformer he gets the following readings. [2]

Supply voltage (V)	Voltmeter reading (V)
2.4	4.8
3.7	7.4
6.2	

There is a gap in the table of readings. Explain why the student could not get a reading to fill this gap.

_____

_____

_____

(d) Suggest two reasons why the student did not use a 240Va.c. supply with this equipment. [2]

1 _____

2 _____

EXAMINER'S COMMENTS

a) You often need to add to diagrams on Paper 3. Make sure you are as clear as possible – use a sharp pencil (and have a sharpener with you in the exam!). You need to draw five turns on the left side of the core in this question to score 1 mark.

(b) Make sure you remember how to connect a voltmeter – in many exam questions candidates lose marks because they forget to connect a voltmeter **in parallel**. In this case, the a.c. supply should be connected across the coil on the **left** of the core (1 mark) with the voltmeter connected across the output coil on the **right** of the core (1 mark).

(c) Now you need to remember what a transformer does! With double the turns on the secondary coil, the output voltage will be twice the input voltage. For an input of 6.2 V the output will be 12.4 V (1 mark) which would be off the scale of the meter (1 mark).

(d) Take care with this part – do not repeat the answer from part (c) about being off the scale. The key point here is that 240 V would be unsafe (1 mark) and the wires or voltmeter could be **damaged / overheated** (1 mark)

2 A circuit is used to see how the resistance of a conducting material varies with its length. The circuit includes a contact **B** which can be moved along the surface of the conducting material. [3]

(a)

B

conducting material

Complete the circuit diagram using the following components.

switch   ammeter   voltmeter

(b) During an experiment a student takes readings from the voltmeter and the ammeter. Record these meter readings. [2]

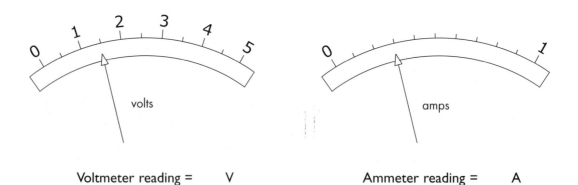

volts   amps

Voltmeter reading =   V   Ammeter reading =   A

(c) The student takes a series of readings and calculates resistance using the formula   [5]

voltage = current × resistance

The table shows her results.

Length (cm)	Resistance (Ω)
2.0	1.3
4.0	2.1
6.0	2.9
8.0	0.27
10.0	4.5

On the grid, plot a graph of resistance (*y*-axis) against length (*x*-axis).

- Label the axes.
- Complete the scales on the axes.
- Plot the points.
- Draw the best straight line. (Note that the best straight line does not go through the origin.)

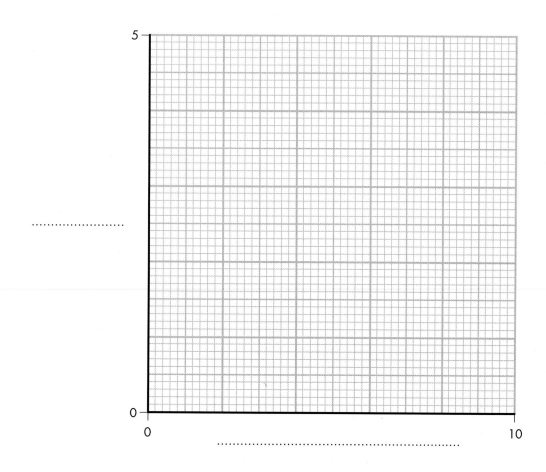

(d) The student retakes readings from the ammeter and voltmeter for a length of 8.0cm. Her readings are the same as before. She has made a mistake in her calculation of resistance.

(i) Read from your graph the 'expected' value of resistance for a length of 8.0cm. [1]

(ii) Suggest the mistake she made in her calculation. [1]

(e) The student used crocodile clips as shown in the diagram.

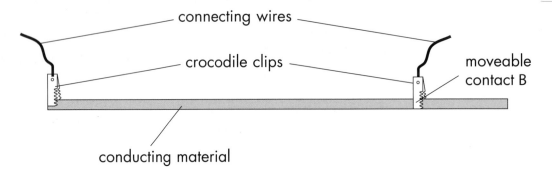

(i) Use your ruler to measure the length in mm of the conducting material between the crocodile clips. [1]

Length = ... mm

(ii) The best straight line on the graph in (c) does not go through the origin. Give a reason for this. [2]

(f) Another student does the experiment but is not concentrating. [2]
His graph is shown below.

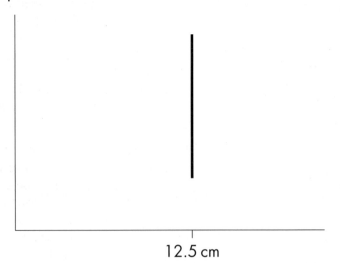

12.5 cm

Suggest what he has done wrong to get this shape of graph.

EXAMINER'S COMMENTS

a) This again tests whether or not you know how to connect basic circuit components. Remember that ammeters are concerned with **how many** electrons are moving, so there are **in series** to measure the electron flow. Voltmeters are concerned with **energy transfers** between two places so they are connected **in parallel**.

In the correct illustration below notice that the switch is in series (1 mark), the ammeter is in series (1 mark) and the voltmeter is in parallel (1 mark).

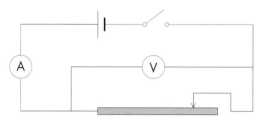

(b) Take care with the scales. For the voltmeter, each division on the scale is 0.5 V, whilst on the ammeter each division is 0.1 A.
Voltmeter reading = 1.5 V (1 mark)
Ammeter reading = 0.3 A (1 mark)

(c) You will almost certainly need to plot some experimental data during the exam. In this example there are five marks available and the question gives four bullet points that you should address – **take the time to think through what information you are given and what you are told to do** – if you follow the instructions carefully you will score most of the marks.

To start with, sort out the **scales on the axes**. The question says the resistance values should be on the y-axis, the **vertical** axis, and the graph already has 0 and 5 marked on to help. There are 5 'large' squares available, so it makes sense to put one ohm per 'large' square. Also note the dotted line given beside the graph - you should add a label saying 'Resistance in ohms'. For the x-axis, the **horizontal** axis, 0 and 10 are already given and you have 5 'large' squares available. On this axis it makes sense to put 2 cm for each 'large' square. Remember to label the axis length in cm.

1 mark is for choosing suitable scales and 1 mark is for labelling the axes with the name of what you are plotting.

Now you need to plot the points accurately. You will gain 2 marks for plotting them all, losing a mark for each mistake you make. You will need to be completely accurate with your plotting.

The final 1 mark is for drawing the best straight line through your points. Remember that you should draw the best line for the **pattern** in the results, which might be a straight line or a curve. In physics we almost never 'join the dots'.

Try to work through a number of questions like this before the examination.

(d) (i) If you have drawn your graph correctly you should read this value in the range 3.6 to 3.7 ohms (1 mark)

(ii) The most common mistake is to calculate resistance = current / voltage, instead of using the correct equation resistance = voltage / current (1 mark)

(e) (i) Measure directly from the exam paper, you gain 1 mark if your answer is in the range 97 to 102 mm. Make sure you put your answer into mm as the question directs.

(ii) Going through the origin would suggest that the resistance was zero when the length of the conducting material was zero (1 mark), but the resistance never was zero because of the resistance of other components (1 mark) such as the crocodile clips, the ammeter, the connecting wires, etc. This is quite a tricky point, so **take time to think an answer through** whenever you can.

(f) For a question like this, you need to think carefully. It is unlikely that you will have seen the particular situation in the question, so you will need to work out a reasonable suggestion. Look at the information you are given - the graph has a range of resistances, but only one length (12.5 cm) is used. **Look back** to the description of the experiment at the start of the question. You would expect the different resistances to be with different lengths, not just one. The value used (12.5 cm) is a little bit longer than those in the table of results – perhaps this is the clue. Now we have a sensible suggestion – this student probably wrote down the whole length of the material (1 mark) for each of the different resistances they measured (1 mark).

ANSWERS

EXAM PRACTICE
Foundation Tier

Q1 **a** (i) microwaves (1)

(ii) infra red (1)

(iii) ultrasonic (1)

Choosing the correct word from a list is very common at this level of question. Notice that all the waves given are part of the electromagnetic spectrum except for ultrasonic. You should know common uses for all parts of the electromagnetic spectrum and for other common waves such as sound / ultrasound.

b (i) B (1)

(ii) A (1)

The wave with the largest amplitude is also the loudest and has the tallest waveform. The wave with the lowest frequency also has the lowest pitch and has the fewest waveforms on the screen.

c disturbance / vibration / movement (1)
direction (1)

Describing the motion in longitudinal waves and transverse waves is tricky, so the examiners have tried to help by giving a sentence to complete and a diagram with some key words. Always look carefully at any diagrams given. Also remember that in a transverse wave the disturbance causing the wave is at right angles to the direction in which the wave moves.

d sound wave (1)

You must remember that sound is an example of a longitudinal wave. Almost all other waves studied at IGCSE are transverse, including all electrmagnetic waves (gamma, X-rays, ultraviolet, visible light, infrared, microwaves and radio waves)

Foundation/Higher Tier Overlap

Q1 **a** A

The air is heated by the convector heater and the hot air will then rise. From the choices available, A will have the highest temperature. The air will be losing heat, and therefore have a lower temperature, as it is moved across to B. The air will only sink to C if it loses more heat and so has an even lower temperature.

b 1.2 (kg/m^3) (3)

Density = mass / volume *or*
volume = area × height (1)

Density = 72 / 60 (1)

Here is a calculation that is worth 3 marks. To get the final answer, you need to calculate the volume of the room (area × height) and then use this number to calculate the density (mass / volume). It is always a good idea to write down your working out. In a situation like this, you need to do two separate calculations and transfer a number between the two. It is very difficult to do all this in your head and, if you try, you increase your chances of making a mistake. Also, as the mark scheme above shows, if you do get the final answer wrong, you may still get some marks for using the correct equations – but only if you show your working out.

c A

The air has the highest temperature at A, so it will have expanded most at that point. If it has expanded the most, then its density will be lowest.

d Conduction

Candidates often get confused when using the terms conduction, convection and radiation. As a general, rough guide – through solids it will be conduction (the particles cannot move), through liquids and gases it will be convection (the particles are mobile). Heat radiation is emitted by any object that is warmer than its surroundings.

Higher Tier

Q1 **a** (i) Alternating current keeps changing direction but direct current flows in a constant direction in a circuit. (1)

This is often answered very poorly, if at all. Common mistakes are to say that 'd.c. (direct current) is a steady current while a.c. (alternating current) is a changing current' – this is wrong. Another common mistake is to give the sources of each (e.g. d.c. from a battery, a.c. from the mains) rather than describing the difference between them.

(ii) Magnet (M) rotates (1), which changes the magnetic field / magnetism / field lines (1) of the iron core (1) and this causes / induces a current in the coil (C) (1).

There are several places in the specification where you need to learn a sequence of events in order. This is one instance. If you learn these parts carefully, you will avoid the common confusions that appear in candidates' answers – it is common to see phrases such as 'magnetic current' and 'the magnet is attracted to the electricity'. Revise carefully before the exam and you will avoid these mistakes.

b (i) Voltage = current × resistance (1)

(ii) $V = 12 - 9 = 3$ V (1)

$R = 3 / 15 = 0.2\ \Omega$ (1)

This question specifically asked for the equation, but make sure you always write the equation anyway. Here, the tricky bit is to realise that the voltage needed is 3 V. However, if you write down your working you will still receive the final mark even if you chose the wrong value for *V*.

Q2 **a** Any two from (1 mark each):

- They are electrons
- They are negative/negatively charged
- They have (almost) zero mass

This is recall using the clues in the nuclear equation given. The symbol given is for an electron, the '0' tells you it has almost no mass, the −1 tells you it is negatively charged. Learn the symbols for alpha, beta and gamma radiation.

b isotopes

This is basic recall. Exam practice cannot help you if you do not spend some time learning basic facts and definitions – make sure you allocate time to do this.

c $^{226}_{88}\text{Ra} \rightarrow\ ^{222}_{86}\text{Rn} + ^{4}_{2}\text{He}$ (1)

You should recognise the symbol for an alpha particle using He. You must learn the numbers that go with it, as mentioned in a) above. Having got these numbers in, you can calculate the numbers for Rn – remember that all the particles must end up somewhere. At the start of the equation there were 88 protons and 226 nucleons, so the totals on the right-hand side of the equation must add up to this.

ANSWERS AND SOLUTIONS

1 FORCES AND MOTION

Movement and position (page 13)

Q1   **a**   speed = distance/time
           = 200 m/20 s = 10 m/s

       b   distance = speed × time
           = 8 m/s × 20 s = 160 m

       c   average speed = total distance/total time
           = 360 m/50 s 7.2 m/s

          In part (c), work out the total distance by adding the 200 m and the 160 m together. Work out the total time by adding up the time for each section – don't forget to include the time waiting at the junction.

Q2   **a**   The speed remained constant.

          If the line on a distance–time graph has a constant gradient then the speed is constant.

       b   600 m

          This can be read off the graph: after 20 s the car had travelled 200 m, after 60 s it had travelled 800 m. So the distance travelled is
          800 – 200 = 600 m.

       c   15 m/s

          Speed = distance/time, v = 600/40 = 15 m/s. Don't forget the units.

       d   It stopped.

          The line is horizontal during this time, indicating that the car was not moving (no distance was travelled).

Q3   **a** $2.0 \ \text{m/s}^2$

          Acceleration = change in velocity/time,
          a = (1.5 – 0)/0.75 = 2 m/s^2

       b   2.25 m

          Total distance = area under the line =
          (1/2 × 0.75 × 1.5) + (1/2 × 2.25 × 1.5) =
          2.25 m

          Note: the tractor showed constant acceleration from A to B and then constant deceleration from B to C.

Forces, movement and shape (page 28)

Q1   **a**   600 N (or 588 N)   **b**   60 kg

       c   228 N   **d**   60 kg

       e   228 N

Q2   **a**   Stay similar   **b**   Increase

       c   Increase   **d**   Increase

       e   Probably stay similar, though there is a case for decrease if, for example, jumping along turned out to be faster than running.

Q3   **a**   Stage 1 – The skydiver is accelerating. The downward force of gravity is greater than the upward force caused by air resistance. Stage 2 – The skydiver is travelling at constant speed. The forces of gravity and air resistance are balanced. Stage 3 – The skydiver is slowing down. The force caused by the air in the parachute is greater than the force of gravity. Stage 4 – The skydiver is travelling at a constant speed. The forces are balanced again.

          In questions of this sort the first thing to do is to decide which forces will be acting on the object. The next thing is to decide whether the forces are balanced or unbalanced. If they are unbalanced the skydiver will be either accelerating or decelerating. If they are balanced the skydiver will either be travelling at constant speed or not moving. In stage 2 the skydiver will have reached the terminal speed and because the forces are balanced will not accelerate or decelerate.

       b   The force of gravity is balanced by the upward force of the ground on the skydiver.

          The upward force from the ground is equal to the skydiver's weight.

Q4   **a**   The graph is a straight line from the origin to the (12 cm, 6.0 N) point. After that it become increasingly curved and less steep. Don't be fooled into drawing a single 'best fit' line as there are two distinct parts to this graph.

       b   The limit of proportionality should be marked on the graph at the end of the region that is a straight line. Proportional behaviour occurs all along the region where the graph is a straight line. Plastic behaviour occurs thereafter, though not necessarily immediately so.

       c   If the spring returns to its original length then the behaviour was purely elastic. If it is longer, then the behaviour was partially elastic and partially plastic.

Q5 **a** 2.5 m/s^2

Acceleration = change in speed/time, $a = (30 - 0)/12 = 2.5 \text{ m/s}^2$. Don't forget the units.

b 2500 N

Force = mass × acceleration, $F = 1000 \times 2.5 = 2500 \text{ N}$.

Q6 **a** 5000 N, approximately north east

b (i) acceleration = force/mass
$= 5000 \text{ N} / 500\,000 \text{ kg} = 0.01 \text{ m/s}^2$

Remember to use the total force that you calculated in part (a).

(ii) change in speed = acceleration × time
$= 0.01 \text{ m/s}^2 \times 10 \text{ s} = 0.1 \text{ m/s}$

Remember that this calculation works out the *change* in the speed, but since the ship has no speed to start with (the question says it is about to start moving) then this is the answer you need.

Q7 800 N m.

Moment = force × distance

Q8 C

C has the widest base and is heavier at the bottom (more glass).

Q9 2 m to the right of the pivot (on Jane's side)

At the moment, Jane's clockwise moment is 300 N × 4 m = 1200 N m.
Freddy's anticlockwise moment is 450 N × 4 m = 1800 N m. Freddy needs to provide a moment of 600 N m clockwise to balance the see-saw. Freddy weighs 300 N, so he needs to sit 2 m from the pivot (300 N × 2 m = 600 N).

2 ELECTRICITY

Mains electricity (page 36)

Q1 **a** 920 W

Power = $V \times I$ = 230 × 4 = 920 W. Don't forget the unit. Power is measured in watts.

b Water greatly increases the hazard of any contact with mains electricity as the skin becomes highly conducting. If the hairdryer is dropped in the washbasin, then any attempt to pick it out will be fatal.

Q2 You should fit an MCB of 30 A. If the supply were 120 V a.c., you should fit an MCB of 40 A.

Energy and potential difference in circuits (page 46)

Q1 **a** A_1 reading 0.2 A, A_2 reading 0.2 A

The current is always the same at any point in a series circuit.

b A_4 reading 0.30 A, A_5 reading 0.15 A

The ammeter A_6 has been placed on one branch of the parallel circuit. Ammeter A_5 is on the other branch. As the lamps are identical the current flowing through them must be the same. Ammeter A_4 gives the current before it 'splits' in half as it flows through the two parallel branches.

Q2 Reading on V_1 = 6 V

The potential difference across the battery is 9 V. This must equal the total p.d. in the circuit. Assuming there is no loss along the copper wiring the p.d. across the lamp must be $9 - 3 = 6$ V.

Q3 **a** Use the equation $I = Q/t$, $I = 10/30 = 0.33$ A.

b (i) 10 C; (ii) 36 000 C

Rearranging the formula, $Q = It$,
(i) $Q = 10 \times 1 = 10$ C,
(ii) $Q = 10 \times 60 \times 60 = 36\,000$ C.

Q4 **a** 24 V

$V = IR = 2 \times 12 = 24$ V

b 20 V

$V = IR = 0.1 \times 200 = 20$ V

c 0.12 A

$I = V/R = 12/100 = 0.12$ A

d 23 A

$I = V/R = 230/10 = 23$ A

e 60 Ω

$R = V/I = 6/0.1 = 60$ Ω

f 23 Ω

$R = V/I = 230/10 = 23$ Ω

Electric charge (page 53)

Q1 **a** Electrons are rubbed off the surface of the plastic onto the cloth.

Static electricity is produced by removing electrons from one insulator to another. An excess of electrons leads to a negative charge.

b The positively charged rod induces a negative charge on the surface of the paper near to the rod. Opposite charges then attract.

Electrostatic induction is a common phenomenon. Remember this is how you can make a balloon stick to the ceiling.

Q2 a The passenger is charged by friction as her clothes rub against the seat covers. The car is also charged by friction with the road and the air. Touching metal allows the charge to flow to earth.

Remember static electricity is produced by friction.

b Touching a door handle after walking on a synthetic carpet, or removing clothing

Synthetic fibres are more likely to cause this effect than natural fibres. This must be due to the different atom arrangements.

Q3 Lightning, fuelling aircraft

Static electricity can cause explosions in any situations when there are fuels in the gaseous form.

3 WAVES

Properties of waves (page 60)

Q1 a The crest is the top of the wave.

b The wavelength is the length of the repeating pattern.

c The amplitude is half the distance between the crest and the trough.

512.

Frequency is measured in hertz and 1 Hz = 1 cycle (or wave) per second.

Q2 0.33 m

$v = f \times \lambda$ or $\lambda = v/f$
$\lambda = 3 \times 10^8 / 9 \times 10^8 = 0.33$ m

Q3 a The water gets shallower 200 m ahead.

b The current is going right to left. The waves make the piece of wood bob up and down, but they do not move it along.

c If this is so, mobile phone signals cannot penetrate the walls of your house and must come in through the windows. Because mobile phones use short wavelengths, the waves cannot easily bend around buildings. Hence unless your window is facing a mobile phone transmitter the signal cannot get to your window.

The electromagnetic spectrum (page 64)

Q1 a Light

The sensitive cells form a part of the eye called the retina.

b Ultraviolet

Suntan lotions contain chemicals that absorb some of the UV radiation from the Sun before it can act on the skin.

c Microwaves

The key word here was 'rapid'. Electric cookers make use of infrared radiation for cooking but microwaves produce much more rapid cooking.

d X-rays

A gamma camera would not be as good for this purpose as the gamma rays penetrate the bone as well as the flesh.

e Infrared

Remote car locking sometimes uses infrared beams.

Q2 a They can pass through soft tissue and kill cancer cells.

Gamma rays are useful because of their great penetrating power. This is also their disadvantage. Consequently they have to be used extremely carefully. They are the highest energy waves in the electromagnetic spectrum.

b They can damage healthy cells and cause cancer because of their very high energy.

As you might have guessed this is an important point and one that is often tested in exams!

c They have different frequencies and wavelengths.

All waves in the electromagnetic spectrum have different frequencies and wavelengths.

d 300 000 000 m/s

All waves in the electromagnetic spectrum travel at the same speed in a vacuum – the speed of light.

Q3 a Radio, microwaves, infrared, visible, ultraviolet, X-rays, gamma

b The order would be reversed.

It is important to learn the spectrum in both directions – textbooks and exam papers sometimes use increasing frequency and sometimes increasing wavelength. Make sure you know which you are dealing with.

Light and sound (page 73)

Q1 **a** In reflection light changes direction when it bounces off a surface. In refraction the light changes direction when it passes from one medium to another.

In reflection the angle of incidence and the angle of reflection are the same. In refraction the angle of incidence does not equal the angle of refraction, as the ray of light bends towards or away from the normal.

b (i)

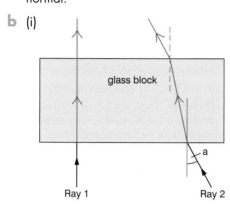

(ii) The angle of incidence

(iii) The normal line

The ray of light will only be bent if it hits the block at an angle. In both cases the speed of the light in the block will be slower than in air.

Q2 **a**

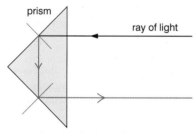

You should draw a normal line to ensure that for each reflection the angles of incidence and reflection are the same.

b Binoculars, bicycle reflector, cat's eyes

Periscopes are also often made using prisms rather than mirrors.

c R, T, T

Total internal reflection occurs only when the angle of incidence is equal to or greater than the critical angle.

Q3 **a** 2.07

b 28.9°

Q4 **a** (i) Vibrations. (ii) Compressions and rarefactions travel through the air.

These are both common questions, so don't forget. Sound is a longitudinal wave. The compressions and rarefactions are small differences in air pressure.

b Sound waves cannot travel through a vacuum. Radio waves don't require a medium.

This is a big difference between sound waves and electromagnetic waves.

c The sound can bend round the buildings and other obstacles between you. In addition, air absorbs high frequencies quite strongly as they travel through it.

Q5 341 m/s (or 340 m/s)

Q6 **a** 1.3 m (or 1.33 m)

b 85 m

4 ENERGY RESOURCES AND ENERGY TRANSFER

Energy transfer (page 87)

Q1 The thin layers will trap air between them. Air is an insulator and so will reduce thermal transfer from the body.

Remember that air is a very good insulator. Trapping it between layers of clothing means that convection is inhibited as well as conduction.

Q2 Energy from the hot water is transferred from the inner to the outer surface of the metal by conduction. Energy is transferred through the still air by radiation.

In a question like this it is important to take the energy transfer stage by stage. Thermal transfer through a solid involves conduction. Thermal transfer through still air must involve radiation. In fact, convection would be occurring and it is very likely that the air behind the radiator would be moving (convention currents).

Work and power (page 91)

Q1 12.5 m

Work done = $F d$
$F = 400 \times 10 = 4000$ N
$d = W/F = 50\ 000/4000 = 12.5$ m

Q2 **a** Energy transferred = 90 J (per step) × 200 (number of steps) = 18 000 J

b Power = energy transferred/time taken = 18 000/180 = 100 W
Remember to convert the time to seconds.

Q3 **a** 10 500 J
G.P.E. = $mgh = 35 \times 10 \times 30 = 10\,500$ J

b 24.5 m/s
Assuming all the potential energy is transferred to kinetic energy:
K.E. = $\frac{1}{2}mv^2$, so v^2 = 2 K.E./m
= 2 × 10 500/35 = 600, and
v = 24.5 m/s

c Some of the gravitational potential energy will have been transferred to thermal energy due to the friction between the sledge and the snow.

Energy must be conserved but friction is a very common cause of energy being wasted, that is, being transferred into less useful forms.

Energy resources and electrical generation (page 94)

Q1 **a** A source that cannot be regenerated – it takes millions of years to form.

A common mistake is to say that it is a source that 'cannot be used again'. Many energy sources cannot be used again but they can be regenerated (e.g. wood).

b Coal, oil and natural gas
These are the fossil fuels. Substances obtained from fossil fuels such as petrol and diesel are not strictly speaking fossil fuels.

c Coal
Coal is becoming increasingly more difficult to mine as more inaccessible coal seams are tackled. The 300 year estimate could be very optimistic.

Q2 **a** The total energy used over this period has increased. There was a reduction in energy used from 1980 to 1983, but since then the consumption has increased.

b The use of oil reduced up until about 1985, but has remained fairly constant since then. The use of coal has reduced as the use of natural gas and nuclear power has increased. The use of hydro power has remained fairly constant. The use of renewables was negligible in 1980, has increased but is still a small percentage of total energy consumption.

c I would expect energy consumption to continue to increase. I would expect the use of renewable energy sources to increase, the use of coal to decrease.

Q3 **a** Any two from: strength of the wind, high ground, constant supply of wind, open ground.

Higher ground tends to be more windy than lower ground. However, the wind farm cannot be built too far away from the centres of population otherwise costs will be incurred in connecting to the National Grid.

b Advantage: renewable energy source, no air pollution. Disadvantage: unsightly, takes up too much space.

Wind turbines can be very efficient. However, they need to be reasonably small and so a large number are needed to generate significant amounts of electricity. Environmentally, although they produce no air pollution they do take up a lot of land.

5 SOLIDS, LIQUIDS AND GASES
Density and pressure (page 106)

Q1 Wood in oil: depends on the sample
Wood in mercury: float
Plastic in oil: depends on the sample
Steel in mercury: float
Silver in air: sink
Gold in mercury: sink
Helium balloon in air: float

Q2 1900 kg/m^3

Q3 If the crown is pure gold, the new water level will be 900 cm^3. If the jeweller has cheated, the water level will be higher than 900 cm^3.

Q4 Ordinary shoe heel = 160 kPa; elephant = 159 kPa; high-heeled shoe = 8000 kPa. The high-heeled shoe will damage the floor.

Q5 He is 15 m deep. If in sea water, the submarine would be slightly less than 15 m deep.

Q6 The increase in pressure is 29.4 kPa. The total pressure is 189.4 kPa.

Change of state (page 112)

Q1 **a** Solids keep their shape because their particles are closely packed together and are held in a rigid shape by the bonds between the particles, whereas the particles in liquids and gases are able to move.

b Gases fill their container because their particles move about freely, whereas the particles in a solid vibrate within their structure and those in a liquid only slide over each other.

Q2 **a** Dish A shows least evaporation, dish B shows more evaporation, and dish C shows most evaporation.

b In dish A, some of the molecules in the water that have high K.E. manage to escape from the surface of the water. In dish B the dish absorbs infrared radiation from the Sun and warms the water. When the temperature of the water increases, the number of water molecules with high K.E. increases and more of them evaporate. In dish C, the just-evaporated water molecules are swept away by the wind and are less likely to return into the water.

c While the water is evaporating, much of the energy absorbed by the dish is carried away by the water molecules with high K.E. When the water has evaporated, this route for the heat energy to escape is blocked and so the heat energy is used to raise the temperature of the dish.

Q3 During evaporation, only a few particles have enough energy to escape from the liquid state to the gas state. In boiling, all the particles have sufficient energy to escape.

Since temperature measures the average energy of the particles, this means that there is a particular temperature – the boiling point – at which all particles have enough energy to escape. In evaporation, the average energy of the particles is lower than this, so evaporation can happen over a range of temperatures – think about a puddle evaporating after it has rained.

Ideal gas molecules (page 118)

Q1 It is the lowest possible temperature, the temperature where the molecules would have zero kinetic energy (and zero speed).

The kinetic theory assumes that no forces act between the particles, except during collisions. In reality, forces do occur between molecules – these would cause the gas to condense to a liquid and then to freeze to a solid at temperatures well above absolute zero. However, the idea behind absolute zero still applies – at absolute zero, the particles in the solid lattice would have zero kinetic energy and all vibration would stop.

Q2 **a** (i) 293 K (ii) 423 K (iii) 1273 K

b (i) 27 °C (ii) 377 °C (iii) 727 °C

Remember:

temperature in °C = temperature in kelvin – 273

temperature in Kelvin = temperature in °C + 273

Q3 1330 cm^3

$$\frac{p_1 V_1}{T_1} = \frac{p_2 V_2}{T_2}$$

In this case, pressure is constant, so the equation becomes $\dfrac{V_1}{T_1} = \dfrac{V_2}{T_2}$

Remember to convert the temperatures to kelvin: 20 °C = 293 K and –13 °C = 260 K

Rewriting the formula in terms of V_2, $V_2 = V_1 T_2/T_1 = (1500 \times 260)/293 = 1330$ cm^3

Working to three significant figures is sufficient.

6 MAGNETISM AND ELECTROMAGNETISM

Magnetism (page 124)

Q1 A magnetically hard material stays magnetic once it has been magnetised (e.g. steel). A magnetically soft material does not stay magnetic when the source of magnetisation is removed (e.g. pure iron).

Q2 The piece of metal could just be made of a soft magnetic material. This will be attracted if it is brought near to a magnet. Ranjit could turn the piece of metal around and see if it is still attracted (in which case it is not a magnet) or repelled (in which case it is a magnet).

Q3 See page 123 for the magnetic field pattern for a single bar magnet. If the magnet were made stronger, the field pattern would not change, but it is common to indicate the increased field strength by drawing more lines between the original ones.

Electromagnetism (page 130)

Q1 Increasing the current flowing through the coil. Increasing the number of coils. Adding a soft iron core inside the cardboard tube.

These will produce a stronger magnetic field.

Q2 When the switch is pressed, the electromagnet attracts the hammer support and the hammer hits the bell. The movement of the hammer support breaks the circuit and so the electromagnet ceases to operate. The hammer support then returns to its original position, forming the circuit again and the process is repeated.

The electromagnet is constantly activated and then deactivated. This means that the hammer will continually hit the bell and then retract.

Electromagnetic induction (page 135)

Q1 **a** Iron

The core must be a magnetic material. It concentrates the magnetic effect.

b A magnetic field is produced.

Remember that a current flowing in a wire will produce a magnetic field around it.

c A current is induced.

The varying magnetic field in the core induces a current in the secondary coil.

d 24 V.

$V_p/V_s = n_p/n_s$; $V_p/14 = 12/7$;
$V_p = 12/7 \times 14 = 24$ V

Q2 If the rotation of the armature is producing electricity which is being withdrawn via A and B, then it is a generator. If, alternatively, electricity is being supplied via A and B to produce rotation, then it is a motor.

The same device can be used as either a motor or a generator. A motor needs an electrical supply in order to produce movement. In a generator the movement is used to generate electricity.

7 RADIOACTIVITY AND PARTICLES

Radioactivity (page 144)

Q1

Atom	Symbol	Number of protons	Number of neutrons	Number of electrons
Hydrogen	$^{1}_{1}H$	1	0	1
Carbon	$^{12}_{6}C$	6	6	6
Calcium	$^{40}_{20}Ca$	20	20	20
Uranium	$^{238}_{92}U$	92	146	92

Remember:
number of electrons = number of neutrons in a neutral atom
number of neutrons = mass number – proton number

Q2 **a** 11 protons, 13 neutrons

The atomic number gives the number of protons. The difference between the mass number and the atomic number equals the number of neutrons.

b 15 hours

The count falls from 100 Bq to 50 Bq in 15 hours. It also falls from 50 Bq to 25 Bq in 15 hours.

Q3 **a** Beta particle

A beta particle is an electron. The 'beta' symbol can also be written as an electron, 'e'. The electron is shown with an atomic number of –1 and a mass number of 0.

b $x = 24$; $y = 12$

The mass numbers must balance on the left-hand and right-hand sides of the equation (24 = 24 + 0). The atomic numbers must balance on the left-hand and right-hand sides of the equation (11 = 12 – 1).

Particles (page 148)

Q1 **a** Alpha particles

b Beta particles

c Gamma rays

Details of these uses are given on page 142. Alpha particles are the most ionising, gamma rays are the most penetrating.

Q2 **a** A tracer is a radioactive isotope used in detection.

Tracers are widely used to detect leaks and blockages.

b Sodium-24. The lawrencium-257 has too short a half-life; the sulphur-35 and carbon-14 have half-lives which are too long.

The tracer must be radioactive for long enough for it to be detected after injection into the body but must not remain radioactive in the body for longer than necessary.

Q3 a Lead

In fact the uranium-238 decays through a chain of short-lived intermediate elements before forming lead.

b The ratio of uranium-238 to lead-207 enables the age of the rock to be determined.

In a similar way the carbon-14: carbon-12 ratio is important in finding out the age of previously living material.

Q4 a Alpha particles

Gamma particles would not have been deflected at all as they are uncharged. Beta particles might work, but they are deflected very easily because they have such a small mass.

b Most of the atom is empty space.

c The atom must have a very high concentration of mass and positive charge. Rutherford called this the nucleus.

The neutron wasn't discovered until 1932.

Q5 All matter is made of atoms, but Geiger and Marsden showed that almost all the volume taken up by an atom is empty – only in a tiny space at the centre (the nucleus) and at some extremely small spots around the centre (the electrons) is there any material at all.

So why can't you just push your hand through all this 'empty space' in the atoms? Because the nucleus and the electrons have electrical properties, which make sure that electrical forces repel you if you try!

GLOSSARY

Passenger jet

Wave in water

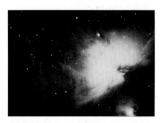

Nebula, some radiation
comes from space

Fair ground ride

Wind power

Thai telephone and power
cables

acceleration How much something's speed increased every second. Acceleration = change in speed / time taken to change.

air resistance Drag caused by something moving through air.

alternating current (a.c.) Electrical current that repeatedly reverses its direction, like mains electricity.

ammeter Instrument that measures electrical current in amperes.

ampere Unit of current. The electric charge that flows during one second.

amplitude Maximum charge of the medium from normal in a wave. For example, the height of a water wave above the level of calm water.

analogue Describes a quantity that can charge smoothly, like the position of a pointer over a dial (the opposite of digital).

background radiation The level of radiation found due to natural processes in the environment.

centripetal force Force that acts towards a centre. A centripetal force is needed to move in a circle.

charge Fundamental property of matter that produces all electrical effects.

compression A region where particles are squashed together.

conductors, heat Substances that conduct heat very well.

conventional current Movement of positive charge that is imagined to move from the positive terminal to the negative terminal of a battery. Equivalent in effect to the real flow of negative charge in the opposite direction.

coulomb Unit of electric charge

crest The highest part of a wave.

current, electric Flowing electric charge.

density The mass, in kilograms, of one metre cube of a substance.

diffraction Waves spreading into the shadow when they pass an edge.

diffusion Molecules moving from an area of high concentration to an area of low concentration.

digital Describes quantities that can only be displayed as numbers (the opposite of analogue).

diode Device that only lets electricity flow through it one way.

direct current (d.c.) Current that always flows in the same direction.

dispersion Splitting white light into colours.

efficiency Ratio of the useful work done by a machine to the energy input, often written as a percentage.

elastic Describes material that go back to their original shape and size after you stretch them.

electric current Flowing electric charge.

electric field Region in which any electrical charges will feel a force.

electromagnetic induction A changing magnetic force can induce electric current in a wire.

electromagnetic spectrum The 'family' of electromagnetic radiations (radio, microwave, infrared, visible light, ultraviolet, X-rays, gamma rays). They all travel at the same speed in a vacuum.

electromagnets Magnets made from a coil of wire. The magnetic force is made when electric current flows in the coil. The magnetic force is stronger when the coil is wrapped around a piece of iron.

electron Negatively charged particles with a negligible mass that form the outer portion of all atoms.

extension The increase in length when something is stretched.

fluid Any liquid or gas.

force A push or a pull, measured in newtons (N).

free fall Movement under the effect of the force of gravity alone.

frequency The number of vibrations per second, measured in hertz (Hz).

friction The force that resists when you try to move something.

fuse A special wire that protects an electric circuit. If the current gets too large, the fuse melts and stops the current.

gamma rays See electromagnetic spectrum

gradient Slope of a curve.

gravitational field strength The force of gravity on a mass of one kilogram. The unit is the newton per kilogram.

gravitational potential energy Objects have more potential energy when they are higher up in the Earth's gravitational field.

half-life Time it takes for half of a sample of radioactive nuclei to decay.

induce To affect something without touching it. An electric force can induce charge in a conductor. A changing magnetic force can induce electric current in a wire.

insulators of heat Substances that do not conduct heat very well.

interference Waves combine with each other as they collide.

ionising radiation Charged particles or high-energy light rays that ionise the material they travel through.

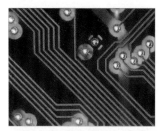

Digital microprocessor

Elastic band ball

End of electrical cable

Satellite dish China

International Space Station

Thailand boat

Astronaut in free fall

Compass

Traditional balance

Electrical circuits in computer

Total eclipse of the sun

Nuclear power plant

inversely proportional Two quantities are inversely proportional if one doubles when the other halves.

joules The unit of energy. One joule is the energy needed to push an object through one metre with a one newton force.

kinetic energy Moving objects have kinetic energy. Fast, massive objects have more kinetic energy than slow light objects.

law of energy, first Energy cannot be created or destroyed.

law of energy, second Some energy always becomes unusable whenever energy is transferred.

longitudinal wave Wave where the change of the medium is parallel to the direction of the wave.

magnetic field Region in which magnetic materials feel a force.

magnetic materials Materials that are attracted to magnets and can be made into magnets. Iron, cobalt, and nickel are magnetic materials.

mass Amount of material in an object, measured in kilograms.

momentum Fast objects and massive objects need a lot of force to stop them – they have a large momentum. Momentum = mass x velocity.

neutron Particle present in the nucleus of atoms that have mass but no charge.

nucleus, atomic The tiny centre of an atom made from protons and neutrons.

Ohm's law The current flowing through a component is proportional to the potential difference between its ends, providing temperature is constant.

parallel Describes a circuit in which the current splits up into more than one path.

photons Particles of light and other electromagnetic radiations. Sometimes radiation behaves like waves, something like particles.

pitch Whether a note sounds high or low to your ear.

polarity Some components only work correctly when connected the right way around – with the right polarity.

potential difference (p.d.) The energy transferred from one coulomb of charge between two points. Measured in volts. Often called the 'voltage'.

power Amount of energy transferred every second. The energy can be transferred from somewhere (e.g. a power station) or to somewhere (e.g. an electric kettle). Power = energy transferred / time taken.

pressure The effect of a force spread out over an area. Pressure = force / area.

primary coil The input coil of a transformer. You connect it to the voltage you want to change.

proton Positively charged, massive particles found in the nucleus of an atom.

radiation Energy that travels in straight lines, e.g. electromagnetic rays.

radioactive decay Natural and random change of a nucleus.

radioactive Describes a substance that has nuclei that are not stable.

rarefaction Region where particles are stretched further apart than normal.

reflection When waves bounce off a mirror. The angle of incidence is the same size as the angle of reflection.

refraction When waves change direction because they have gone into a different medium. They change direction because their speed changes.

resistance Property of an electrical conductor that limits how easily an electric current flows through it. Measured in ohms.

resultant force A single imaginary force that is equivalent to all the forces acting on an object.

series Describes a circuit in which the current travels along one path through every component.

short circuit Unwanted branch of an electrical circuit that bypasses other parts of the circuit and causes a large current to flow.

speed How far something moves every second. Average speed = distance travelled / time taken.

spectrum The 'rainbow' of colours that make up white light (red, orange, yellow, green, blue, indigo and violet).

transformer Machine that changes the voltage of a.c. electricity.

transverse wave A wave where the change of the medium is at 90 (degrees) to the direction of the wave.

trough Lowest part of a wave.

variable resistor Component with a resistance that can be manually altered.

velocity Quantity that indicates the speed and direction of an object.

volt Unit of voltage. Energy carried by one coulomb of electric charge.

watt Unit of power. One watt is one joule transferred every second.

wave equation Wave speed = frequency x wavelength.

wavelength The distance between the same points of successive waves. For example, the distance from one crest to the next.

weight Force of gravity on a mass. The unit of weight is the Newton.

work Energy transferred when a job is done. Work = force x distance moved in direction of force.

Bangkok bridge

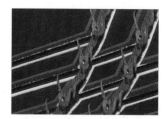

Roof south east Asia

Mobile phone

Spectrum as rainbow

Transformer

Southeast Asia weight

INDEX

Acknowledgements

The Authors and Publishers are grateful to the following for permission to reproduce copyright material:

Edexcel Ltd: pp 153 – 172
Edexcel Ltd accept no responsibility whatsoever for the accuracy or method of working in the answers given.

Photographs

Jupiterimages Corporation (c) 2006 8, 9, 20, 21, 37, 51, 56, 59, 63, 65, 70, 78, 79, 87, 92, 93, 98, 99, 100, 101, 102, 104, 105, 108, 112, 114, 122, 127, 134, 135, 138, 143, 146, 147, 184 - 187; Andrew Lambert 32; Pbase 49; Science Photo Library 62; David Vincent 4, 101, 103, 123, 125, 128, 129

Cover: Newton's cradle – DK Images Tim Ridley © Dorling Kindersley

Inside Front Cover spread: Isaac Newton – Photo Researchers/ Science Photo Library; Newton's cradle – Martyn F Chillmaid/ Science Photo Library; bouncing ball – Adam Hart-Davis/Science Photo Library; Einstein – US Library of Congress/Science Photo Library

Section spreads: pp6/7 petronas towers – © Jose Fuste Raga/ Corbis; Taipei 101 – © Simon Kwong/Reuters/Corbis; pp30/31 new Honda hybrid system, cutaway model – Curtesy Honda; pp54/55 Artwork showing Envisat-1 satellite in orbit – European Space Agency/Science Photo Library; Singapore and surroundings – NASA/Science Photo Library; pp76/66 wind trubines – Mark Thomas/Science Photo Library; pp96/97 succulent plants – Andrew McRobb/DK Images © Dorling Kindersley; pp120/121 arctic tern – © Arthur Morris/Birds As Art/NHMPL; Earth's magnetic field – Gary Hincks/Science Photo Library; pp136/137 Gamma scan of skull & spine showing bone cancer – Philippe Plailly/Science Photo Library

Every effort has been made to contact the holders of copyright material, but if any have been inadvertently overlooked, the Publishers will be pleased to make the necessary arrangements at the first opportunity.